Dutch Reformed Theology

Reformed Theology in America
Edited by David F. Wells

Dutch Reformed Theology

Edited by
David F. Wells

 **BAKER BOOK HOUSE**
Grand Rapids, Michigan 49516

Copyright 1989 by
Baker Book House Company

The material in this volume originally comprised part of a book titled *Reformed Theology in America: A History of Its Modern Development*, copyright 1985 by Wm. B. Eerdmans Publishing Company.

Printed in the United States of America

Library of Congress Cataloging-in-Publication Data

Dutch Reformed theology / edited by David F. Wells
    p. cm.
"The material in this volume originally comprised part of a book titled Reformed theology in America: a history of its modern development, copyright 1985 by Wm. B. Eerdmans Publishing Company"—T.p. verso.
Other portions of this original work republished under Southern Reformed theology and Princeton theology.
    Bibliography: p.
    Includes index.
    Contents: The Dutch schools / James D. Bratt—Louis Berkhof / Henry Zwaanstra—Herman Dooyeweerd in North America / C.T. McIntire—Cornelius Van Til / Wesley A. Roberts.
    ISBN 0-8010-9701-0
    1. Reformed Church—United States—Doctrines—History. 2. Presbyterian Church—United States—Doctrines—History. 3. Calvinism—United States—History. 4. Theology, Doctrinal—United States—History. 5. Theologians—United States—History. I. Wells, David F. II. Reformed theology in America.
BX9424.5.U6D88   1989   89-6914
                                                                     CIP

To Roger Nicole
A man of God

CONTENTS

CONTRIBUTORS

James D. Bratt is assistant professor of history, Calvin College, and author of *Dutch Calvinism in Modern America: A History of a Conservative Subculture* (Grand Rapids: Eerdmans, 1984).

George M. Marsden, professor of the history of Christianity in America at The Divinity School, Duke University, is the author of *Reforming Fundamentalism: Fuller Seminary and the New Evangelicalism* (Grand Rapids: Eerdmans, 1984), *Fundamentalism and American Culture* (New York: Oxford University Press, 1980), and *The Evangelical Mind and the New School Presbyterian Experience* (New Haven: Yale University Press, 1970); coauthor (with Mark Noll and Nathan Hatch) of *The Search for Christian America* (Westchester, IL: Crossway, 1983); and editor of *Evangelicalism and Modern America* (Grand Rapids: Eerdmans, 1984).

C. T. McIntire, associate professor of history, Trinity College, University of Toronto, has edited *God, History, and Historians* (New York: Oxford University Press, 1977), *Herbert Butterfield: Writings on Christianity and History* (New York: Oxford University Press, 1979), and *History and Historical Understanding* (Grand Rapids: Eerdmans, 1984). He also is the author of *England Against the Papacy, 1858–1861* (Cambridge: Cambridge University Press, 1983).

Wesley A. Roberts, formerly professor of church history at Gordon-Conwell Theological Seminary, is now pastor of Peoples Baptist Church of Boston.

Henry Zwaanstra is professor of historical theology at Calvin Theological Seminary and the author of *Reformed Thought and Experience in a New World: A Study of the Christian Reformed Church and Its American Environment, 1890–1918* (Kampen: J. H. Kok B.V., 1973).

PREFACE

ONE of the quirks of American theology is that it is frequently unaware of being American. German theology, of course, is the result of the ponderous and enormously thorough German academic machinery from which it has emerged. British theology, with its keen interest in historical accuracy, fair play, and civility, obviously reflects the virtues of the middle and upper-middle classes in which it is largely nurtured. South American theology makes no bones about being South American. It wears its heart on its sleeve. North of the border, however, this is not so. Here, we simply do theology!

If that were really true, then we should expect to find in the various expressions of Reformed theology a striking conformity, for they are all disciplined by the Reformation principles of *sola Scriptura, sola gratia, in solo Christo,* and *sola fide.* What we actually encounter is a most astonishing variety of expression, despite the common ownership of these principles. Immigrants who have come to these shores, nurturing within themselves the Reformed faith on which they were reared, did not melt into the national pot as they were supposed to. Ethnic interests, in fact, were often preserved through language and custom even as a diffuse sense of what it meant to be American also grew in importance. And, along the way, Reformed theologies have struck up alliances with the habits of mind that have prevailed in this or that age as well as being shaped by the towering figures who, from time to time, have arisen above the tradition and given it new cogency, new direction, and sometimes new horizons. American Reformed theology, as a result, is a complex tradition made up of strands and tributaries that are not only diverse but also sometimes quite oblivious to one another.

In 1985 *Reformed Theology in America: A History of Its Modern Development* appeared. To those with eyes to see, it was a thinly disguised *Festschrift* for Roger Nicole, who was celebrating his seventieth birthday that year. But it was also a serious accounting of the Reformed tradition in all of its diversity. I chose what I saw to be the five major streams of Reformed thought: the Princeton theology, the Westminster school, the Dutch schools, the Southern tradition, and neoorthodoxy. Within each of these sections I followed the same pattern of providing readers with a general essay on the school and essays on its two most prominent theologians.

The success that attended the publication of this study was nowhere better attested than in the dozens of letters I received, as well as in the reviews which were published, that complained about this or that group which had been excluded from consideration! All of a sudden I was beset with the knowledge of numerous groups, streams, traditions, and movements that would have liked to have been recognized and felt a little aggrieved that I had not seen fit to include them! It was then that I knew that I had to seek a new publisher for this work once the Eerdmans edition had run its course.

I am deeply grateful for the willingness of Baker Book House to do this. They decided to divide the original study into three smaller books, representing the sections originally published as the Princeton theology, the Dutch schools, and the Southern tradition. (Two essays from the Westminster section—J. Gresham Machen and Cornelius Van Til—have been included with Princeton theology and Dutch schools respectively.) To each volume is appended George Marsden's introduction, and to each is added a bibliography, which was not in the original edition. I wish to thank James Bratt (the Dutch schools), William Yount (the Southern tradition), and Mark Noll (the Princeton theology) for their excellent work.

These three studies will be of particular interest to those who identify themselves with these traditions. I hope, however, that in addition to this anticipated readership there will be many others who look with fresh interest on these works. Those who care about the church, who treat their faith with seriousness, and who long that God's greatness, his sufficiency, and his glory would be more widely owned and celebrated, can only watch the current developments in the evangelical world with growing disquiet. Evangelical faith is showing too many signs of having become secularized, of fragmenting, of regressing to a stage of immaturity that surely raises the question as to how long it can survive as recognizably evangelical in the midst of the furnace of modernity. In the Reformation traditions there is a strength, a virility, a power of correction that needs to be heard again in today's evangelical world, and it is my prayer that in some small way these volumes may contribute to that end.

D.F.W.
Easter, 1989

INTRODUCTION: REFORMED AND AMERICAN

GEORGE M. MARSDEN

WHAT sense does it make in late twentieth-century America to talk about being "Reformed"? For most Americans the word conveys no clear meaning. Very few would think of it as a religious designation at all, and most of those would think it referred to Judaism. Even if, as in the present work, we limit the audience to those who have some notion of "Reformed theology," we are left with the problem that even among such a select group, "Reformed" has numerous differing connotations. In the United States alone there are about a dozen Reformed denominations and perhaps another half-dozen with a Reformed heritage. Within each of the Reformed denominations varieties of meanings are given to being "Reformed." These may reflect European traditions, such as Scottish or Dutch, or continental neoorthodox, as well as a variety of American developments. Each such type includes differing subtypes. For instance, within the Reformed Church in America alone, ten distinct approaches to the Reformed faith have been identified.[1] Differences across denominational lines may be sharper. A strictly confessional member of the Reformed Presbyterian Church in North America (Covenanters) might be most unhappy with the preaching at Robert Schuller's Crystal Cathedral. A fundamentalist Bible Presbyterian would refuse fellowship with almost any member of the United Church of Christ. And within most of the larger Reformed denominations, conservatives and progressives are locked in intense struggles over the true meaning of the faith.

A major purpose of this essay is to cut through the bewildering confusion of the many meanings of "Reformed" by reducing the categories to the three major Reformed emphases that have flourished in the American cultural setting. Not every Reformed heritage can be subsumed under these categories and the categories are ideal types or models rather than fully nuanced representations of the growth of each type. Nonetheless, these are the major subgroups that have been prominent among the Reformed throughout American history. So if we understand some-

1

thing of these three developments and emphases we can gain a fairly good picture of the main varieties of being "Reformed" in the American cultural setting.

Perhaps an illustration from my own experience can make clear the characters of the differences among these major American Reformed traditions. Most of my life I have lived in one or the other of two communities that placed great merit on being Reformed. The central meaning of "Reformed," however, has differed greatly in these two communions. The Orthodox Presbyterians, among whom I was reared, meant by "Reformed" strict adherence to Christian doctrine as contained in the infallible Scriptures and defined by the standards of the Westminster Assembly. Only Christians whose creeds were fully compatible with Westminster's and who viewed subscription to them as paramount were fully within the pale. Other factors were important to Christian life, especially a proper emphasis on the law of God as the central organizing principle in the Westminster formulations. But the operative test for "Reformed" was, with this important practical proviso, always doctrinal.

In the other community in which I have spent many years, the progressive wing of the conservative Christian Reformed Church, being "Reformed" is also taken seriously, but with very different meaning. There, a "Reformed" Christian is one who has a certain view of the relationship of Christianity to culture. She or he must affirm the lordship of Christ over all reality, see Christian principles as applicable to all areas of life, and view every calling as sacred. Although subscription to the authority of the Bible and classic Reformed creeds is significant in this community, the stronger operative test for admission is support for separate Christian schools at all levels (except, oddly, the graduate university), where the "Reformed" world-and-life view can be exemplified and taught.

I have also spent some time at institutions of mainstream American evangelicalism, such as Trinity Evangelical Divinity School and Fuller Theological Seminary, where one finds still another meaning to being "Reformed." In this context being "Reformed" must be understood in the framework of being "evangelical." "Evangelical" is a word with a more elusive meaning than "Reformed." Basically it refers to anyone who promotes proclamation of the gospel of salvation through the atoning work of Christ and has a traditional high view of Scripture alone as authority. Evangelicalism is thus much larger than just the Reformed tradition. Within American evangelicalism, however, there is an important subgroup that might be called "card-carrying" evangelicals.[2] These are persons who think of themselves primarily as "evangelicals" and who, as such, identify at least as much with evangelicalism as a movement as with their own formal denomination. Billy Graham, *Christianity*

Today, Eternity, Inter-Varsity Christian Fellowship, Wheaton College and its imitators, and seminaries such as Trinity, Fuller, and Gordon-Conwell have been prototypes of this influential interdenominational evangelicalism. In this evangelical fellowship the dominant theological tradition is Reformed. It is by no means, however, the only tradition. One trait of this type of being "Reformed," unlike the other two, is that it is tolerant of diversity to the point of keeping close fellowship with persons of other traditions. The operative tests for fellowship among the Reformed in such communities are those of the broader American evangelical-pietist tradition—a certain style of emphasis on evangelism, personal devotions, Methodist mores, and openness in expressing one's evangelical commitment. To be "Reformed" in this setting means to find in Reformed theology the most biblical and healthiest expression of evangelical piety.

The differing emphases of these three communities suggest that in America there are at least three major meanings to being "Reformed." There are, of course, also a number of other Reformed traditions and styles in America. These include the southern, ethnically and racially defined groups, smaller denominations, progressive Reformed in mainline denominations, and some neoorthodox. Nonetheless, the three we have begun with suggest classically distinct types of emphasis that give us some working categories. Many of the developments of America's Reformed groups can be understood as variations on these typical themes.

For convenience' sake, we shall designate these three types as doctrinalist, culturalist, and pietist.[3] In doing so, it is important to remark again that the terminology refers to "ideal types" or descriptive models emphasizing one dominant trait. In reality all three groups typically embody the traits dominant among the other two. Thus a "pietist" is not typically a person who is lax in doctrine or lacking in cultural concern. Similarly, to call people doctrinalists or culturalists does not imply lack of the other two traits.

The Puritan Stock

The oldest major Reformed community in America was the Puritan, which combined strong elements of each of these emphases. Stress on strict Calvinism helped distinguish these early American settlers from their Arminian Anglican opponents. And Reformed orthodoxy was retained in most New England pulpits for at least a century and a half, to the time of the Revolution.[4] Puritans were also characterized by intense piety, often keeping close records of their spiritual health. Moreover, New England's Puritans were America's most successful Reformed culture builders. Virtually free from outside control during their formative first half-century, they built the closest thing humanly possible to their conception of a biblical kingdom. This impressive effort had a lasting impact on the ideals of American civilization. It is ironic that "Reformed" has so little meaning in America today when in fact the culture has been so shaped by that heritage.

The lasting culture-shaping impact of seventeenth-century Puritanism is rivaled by the long-term influence of its eighteenth-century style of piety, epitomized by the Great Awakening. The eighteenth century was generally an era of widespread resurgent pietism, emphasizing personal commitment to the Savior more than Christian culture building. The Great Awakening in New England was part of a wider Protestant pietist awakening that had begun in Germany and spread to most of the Protestant world. In England its largest manifestation was in Methodism. In America it appeared first primarily as pietist revivalism in Reformed churches.

At the height of the first surge of the Great Awakening in America, around 1740, the classic patterns of American Reformed divisions began to emerge. By this time the other major Reformed group, the Scotch-Irish and Scottish Presbyterian, was on the scene. The often changing relations of the Scottish churches to the state, and the sometimes troubled colonial experiences of the Scotch-Irish in the north of Ireland, fostered among Presbyterians in America varieties of views, or perhaps an ambivalence, concerning culture shaping. They inherited the Calvinist impulse to establish a Christian commonwealth; but they also had enough experience of religious oppression to be suspicious of religious establishments, especially when they were living, as in America, under British rule. The Christian commonwealth would be built by persuasion and education.[5]

The symbol of Presbyterian distinctiveness and unity was thus not a social-political program (except that they were militantly anti-British during the Revolution) but doctrinal orthodoxy. Strict confessionalism was a major trait of the largest party of Scotch-Irish and Scottish Presbyterians from their first appearance in the colonies. Presbyterianism in America, however, was from the outset fed by some other streams, not of Scottish but of English origin. English Presbyterianism itself had become tolerant of doctrinal diversity by the early eighteenth century. More importantly, New England Puritans, especially those in Connecticut, viewed themselves as close allies of Presbyterianism in the Middle Colonies and in the early eighteenth century were providing the newly formed (ca. 1706) Presbyterian Church with personnel and leaders. By the time of the Great Awakening, the New England party was closely linked with the more pietistic revivalist group of the Presbyterians. In

1741 this revivalist "New Side" group split from the antirevivalist Scotch-Irish or Scottish "Old Side." Remarkably, these two Presbyterian "sides" reunited in 1758, thus suggesting that pietist revivalism and doctrinalist confessionalism were compatible. But the tension between these two emphases repeatedly reemerged. The classic instance was in the Old School/New School schism of 1837-38, in many ways a repetition of the Old Side/New Side conflict. The Old School was clearly the stronghold of Scotch-Irish and Scottish elements and found its unity in strict confessionalism. The New School, on the other hand, represented an alliance of more strongly pietist or prorevivalist Presbyterians with New England Congregationalists.

The Growth of Reformed Branches

By this time, however, a number of other issues surrounded this renewed confrontation between confessionalist and pietist axes. The New School was the more typically American of the two groups, its distinctive characteristics reflecting the tendencies of the ethos of the dominant American evangelicalism. This meant that they were more tolerant of theological innovation and variety than had been their predecessors in the seventeenth- and eighteenth-century American Reformed camps. This doctrinal latitude, however, was not a liberalism that involved intentional concessions to secularism (as in later modernism). Rather, it was an outgrowth of pietist zeal for revivalism. In politically liberal America, such zeal translated into some mildly anti-Calvinist (or semi-Pelagian) doctrines emphasizing an unaided human ability voluntarily to accept the revivalists' gospel message with its culminating summons of "choose ye this day." Such doctrinal innovations were held more closely in check by the New School Presbyterians than by their revivalist Congregationalist allies, such as Charles G. Finney. Moreover, they propounded these innovations in the name of greater faithfulness to Scripture alone, as opposed to what some saw as an unhealthly traditionalism of the Old School.

Openness to practical innovation also characterized the New School pietist strand of the heritage. Finney's "New Measures" for promoting revival in the manner of the high-pressure salesman were only the most prominent examples of evangelicalism's openness to departures from tradition. The spread of gospel music perhaps best exemplified the new evangelical style. Especially notable was a new emphasis on personal experience. Controversial also among the Presbyterians was the New School enthusiasm for working through ecclesiastically independent societies (what are now called parachurch agencies) for missions, evangelism, publication, education, and social reform.

This latter issue of social reform was creating a new source of controversy concerning what it meant to be "Reformed," a debate over what we are calling its culturalist heritage. Prior to the nineteenth century, questions concerning social reform had not been conspicuous, divisive issues. Until that time almost all the Reformed groups seem to have been working on the basis of a vaguely formulated, but deeply entrenched, tradition that, ideally, the religion of a nation should be exclusively Reformed. So they assumed that being Reformed accordingly involved transforming the moral ethos and legal system of a people so that it should comport with God's law. The Puritans, as we have seen, worked these principles out most fully in practice. By the early nineteenth century, however, these Reformed principles had to be translated to fit a pluralistic and democratic situation. The question therefore became that of how much emphasis the Reformed Churches should put on shaping the legal structures of a society they did not otherwise control. Was it not the case that the true mission of the church was to proclaim a pure gospel and be a model moral subcommunity within the larger community, leavening it rather than attempting to legislate morality for all?

Finding answers to these questions was complicated by the fact that sometimes the resolution to moral issues could have as much to do with where one stood politically as it did what theological principles one held. Thus, whereas regarding Sabbath observance most nineteenth-century Reformed groups could unite in supporting legislation, on the issue of slavery they were sharply divided. Moreover, opinions on the slavery issue varied strikingly with geography. In the deep South, Reformed people were adamantly opposed to any interference with the practice of black slavery and emphasized aspects of the tradition that favored confining the activities of the church to strictly "spiritual" issues. In New England, by contrast, Reformed Christians often took the lead in insisting that the churches should unrelentingly urge the state to enact immediate emancipation. In the upper South and the lower North, opinions were more varied and often more nuanced. New School Presbyterian leaders, having New England connections, were typically moderate antislavery types, while the Old School sided with the theologically conservative South in wanting to sidestep this and other social reform issues.

"Old School" and "New School" outlooks had thus emerged as the two leading American patterns of being Reformed. The Old School was most characteristically doctrinalist, while the more innovative New School combined pietist revivalism with a culturalist emphasis, inherited from the Puritans, looking for a Christianization of American life. These divisions were not confined to Presbyterians, although they took their clearest shape among them. A number of smaller denominations, including some Baptists, were strictly Reformed doctrinalist groups. Other groups, among whom were some Baptists, the Reformed Church in America, and especially the majority of New England's Congregationalists, were clearly in the New School camp and part of the Reformed wing of the formidable American evangelical coalition that stressed pietism and culturalism. Through the Civil War era, these two schools of Reformed were not irreconcilable, especially once the slavery issue was removed. Most notably, after the war, in 1869 the New School and Old School Presbyterians in the North reunited.

The South, on the other hand, remained separate, holding on to its predominantly Old School tradition and urging the church to stay out of politics. Ironically this apolitical stance of the southern church was deeply mixed with defense of the southern way of life. Accordingly, during the next century the Old School doctrinalism of the Southern Presbyterians was associated with (at least local) cultural influence. In the North, on the other hand, confessionalism lost much of its social base and became more and more associated with a remnant mentality.

The New School heritage, on the other hand, emerged by the end of the century as the stronger of the two traditions in the North. The New School, however, was a combination of two emphases, pietist and culturalist, and these were separable. The divorce between them occurred under the pressures associated with the rapid modernization and secularization of American life between 1870 and 1930. Industrialization, urbanization, immigration, and pluralization undermined the social basis for the old evangelical (and often Reformed) religious quasi-establishment. Moreover, liberal democratic ideology, emphasizing human freedom, ability, and essential goodness, undermined the distinctly Calvinist doctrines. Even more basically, the new naturalistic science and history of the day challenged the authority of the Bible.

Broadly considered, evangelical Christians who responded to these crises moved in one of two directions. One group adjusted to modern times by toning down the supernaturalistic aspects of the gospel and stressing rather those parts of the Christian message that could be realized by developing natural (although God-given) human individual or cultural potentials. On the other side, conservatives reemphasized the fundamentals of the faith, which stressed God's supernatural interventions into history. Thus in the Reformed communities, as in many other areas of American life, a new division was superimposed on existing patterns.

The modernist accommodations to prevailing ideas and ideals fit least well with doctrinalist emphases and best with culturalist. Such theological liberalism was in principle compatible with some pietist emphases (as in a romantic religion of the heart), but in the long run piety proved difficult to sustain from generation to generation without a strong sense of radical divine intervention.

In the New School traditions (including Presbyterian, Congregationalist, Reformed Church in America, Baptist, and other heirs of the nineteenth-century evangelical mainstream), where doctrinalism was not especially strong, the new liberalism flourished, at least among some of the denominational leadership. It grew first, in the late Victorian era, as a version of evangelical romantic piety. In the progressive era, following the turn of the century, it also blossomed as part of the theological basis for the social gospel movement. By this time liberal Protestantism was moving away from crucial parts of traditional evangelical doctrine, repudiating emphases on personal salvation through trust in Christ's work of substitutionary atonement and rejecting the infallibility and reliability of Scripture. These liberal notions alarmed some of the heirs to revivalist pietism. Ecclesiastical warfare broke out and eventually brought a long series of splits between the two camps. Since the social gospel was associated with the modernist tendencies, the "fundamentalist" opponents tended to reject all "social gospels," or culturalist emphases. Such rejections, however, were seldom consistently sustained. New School revivalists also had a heritage of aspiring to Christianize America on a voluntary basis. Thus even when, especially after about 1920, fundamentalists decried the social gospel, they typically still endorsed a politically conservative culturalism that involved efforts to return America to nineteenth-century evangelical standards, as was seen in the anti-evolution and prohibition movements.

The supernaturalist or fundamentalist party among the Reformed included major elements of Old School or doctrinalist heritage as well as the successors to New School evangelicalism. The Old School party, centered first at Princeton Theological Seminary and after 1929 at Westminster Theological Seminary, provided intellectual foundations for defending the traditional faith. The common enemy, modernism, brought these strict confessionalists into close alliance with Reformed people of more New School or pietist-revivalist heritage for a time. Thus by the early 1930s the strictly confessionalist Presbyterians who followed New Testament scholar and apologist J. Gresham Machen were closely allied with Presbyterians among the more strictly revivalist fundamentalists, such as those at Wheaton College or Moody Bible Institute.

The groupings among these theologically Reformed fundamentalists were complicated by the presence of still another major new camp— the dispensationalists. Dispensationalism was essentially Reformed in its nineteenth-century origins and had in later nineteenth-century America spread most among revival-oriented Calvinists. Strict Old School confessionalists were, however, uneasy with dispensationalists' separation of the Old Testament dispensation of Law from the era of Grace in the church age. Dispensationalism, accordingly, was accepted most readily by Reformed Christians who had a more New School, or revivalist-evangelical, emphasis than among the various Old School, or doctrinalist, groups. During the fundamentalist controversies, however, these two groups were thrown into each other's arms.

The union, however, did not last. In 1937 the followers of Machen who had just left the Presbyterian Church in the U.S.A. split roughly into Old School and New School camps, with the more revivalist group, led by Carl McIntire, favoring dispensationalism and total abstinence from alcoholic beverages. About the same time, doctrinalist Southern Presbyerians took a stand against dispensationalism in their denomination.

Another, less separatist branch of the New School evangelical party survived well in the "new evangelicalism" that grew out of fundamentalism after World War II. The new evangelicals were largely Reformed in leadership and had moved away from strict dispensationalism. Institutionally they gained strength at centers such as Wheaton College, Fuller Theological Seminary, Trinity Evangelical Divinity School, and Gordon-Conwell Theological Seminary. *Christianity Today*, founded in 1956 under the editorship of Carl F. H. Henry, gave them wide visibility and influence. Inter-Varsity Christian Fellowship, InterVarsity Press, and the ministry of Francis Schaeffer also added substantially to the outreach of this Reformed evangelicalism. Keeping cordial relations with many individuals and groups not Reformed and with evangelicals both within and outside mainline denominations, this New School tradition has emerged as one of the most influential expressions of evangelicalism today.

The Old School, though smaller, also remains active. It has wide influence through Westminster Theological Seminary and similar conservative schools. Denominationally, it is especially strong in the Presbyterian Church of America and in the conservative wing of the Christian Reformed Church. It is also found among Reformed Baptists and in other smaller Reformed denominations.

Of the three strands of the heritage, the culturalist emphasis is the least unified today. Nonetheless, it is perhaps as prominent as it ever has been. This continuing emphasis, that Calvinists should be transforming culture and bringing all of creation back to its proper relationship to God's law, has been resurgent due to the convergence of a number of developments. Most clearly articulating these views have been the North American Kuyperians, followers of the turn-of-the-century Dutch theologian and politician, Abraham Kuyper. Kuyperianism was brought to America largely by the Dutch-American Christian Reformed Church, where a hard-line Kuyperianism also developed among the admirers of

Dutch philosopher Herman Dooyeweerd. Dooyeweerdianism has en-
listed non-Dutch disciples, but the widest influence of Kuyperianism
spread in a mild form through the neoevangelical movement after World
War II. The fundamentalist tradition, said neoevangelical spokespersons
such as Carl F. H. Henry, had not sufficiently recognized that the Christian task involves relating a Christian "World-and-life view" to all of
culture and politics.[6]

By the 1970s such moderately conservative emphases were con-
verging with the resurgence of conservative politics among American
fundamentalists and fundamentalistic evangelicals. Fundamentalists had
their own, vaguely Reformed, traditions of wanting to Christianize
America. Versions of Kuyperian Calvinism such as those suggested by
Francis Schaeffer in the influential political ministry of his later years
helped articulate the new fundamentalist conservative political emphases
of the Moral Majority. Schaeffer drew many of his political ideas from
the work of the politically conservative Dooyeweerdian thinker, Rousas J.
Rushdoony. Rushdoony also contributed to the emergence of the hyper-
Reformed "theonomist" movement, which insists that Old Testament
law should be the basis of American civil law.

The irony in this resurgence of Reformed culturalism is that the
culturalists, who are often united in theological theory, are so deeply
divided in practice. Cutting across the culturalist movement is a seem-
ingly insurmountable divide between those who are politically conservative and those who are politically liberal. Many of the American
followers of Kuyper have been politically liberal and these had an impact
on the politically progressive evangelicalism that emerged during the
1960s and early 1970s.[7] Moreover, the politically liberal Reformed culturalist camp includes Reformed Christians in mainline denominations
whose traditions still reflect the political progressivism of the social gospel days. In addition, the neoorthodox heritage in such denominations
has contributed, especially via the work of H. Richard Niebuhr and
Reinhold Niebuhr, to generally Reformed culturalist sensibilities tem-
pered by a Lutheran sense of the ambiguities inherent in relating Christianity to an essentially pagan culture.

The American Reformed community today, then, still includes substantial representation of the three classic emphases, doctrinalism, pietism, and culturalism. These three are, of course, not incompatible and
the unity of Reformed Christians in America would be much greater
were this compatibility recognized and emphasized.

The question of unity, however, is complicated by the twentieth-
century divisions of modernists and fundamentalists that have cut across
the traditional divisions. Neoorthodox and dispensationalist variations

add further complications. Moreover, among those who are primarily culturalists, conflicting political allegiances subvert Reformed unity. Nonetheless, there remain a substantial number of Reformed Christians whose faith reflects a balance, or potential balance, of the three traditional emphases. It is these Christians who need to find each other and who might benefit from reflecting on what it should mean to be Reformed. They can also learn from considering the characteristic weaknesses, as well as the strengths, of their tradition. Perhaps the greatest fault of American Reformed communities since Puritan times is that they have cultivated an elitism. Ironically, the doctrine of election has been unwittingly construed as meaning that Reformed people have been endowed with superior theological, spiritual, or moral merit by God himself. The great irony of this is that the genius of the Reformed faith has been its uncompromising emphasis on God's grace, with the corollary that our own feeble efforts are accepted, not because of any merit, but solely due to God's grace and Christ's work. The doctrine of grace, then, ought to cultivate humility as a conspicuous trait of Reformed spirituality. A strong sense of our own inadequacies is an important asset for giving us positive appreciation of those who differ from us.

Yet too often Reformed people have been so totally confident of their own spiritual insights that they have been unable to accept or work with fellow Reformed Christians whose emphases may vary slightly. Perhaps some review of the rich varieties of theological views among the Reformed in America today will contribute to bringing tolerance and search for balance. Moreover, the unmistakable minority status of the "Reformed" in America today should help foster the need for mutual understanding and respect. Above all, however, a revival of the central Reformed distinctive—the sense of our own unworthiness and of total dependence on God's grace, as revealed especially through Christ's sacrificial work—should bring together many who in late twentieth-century America still find it meaningful to say "I am Reformed."

Notes: Reformed and American

1. I. John Hesselink, *On Being Reformed: Distinctive Characteristics and Common Misunderstandings* (Ann Arbor: Servant Books, 1983), 2 and 113.

2. This concept is elaborated in *Evangelicalism and Modern America*, ed. George M. Marsden (Grand Rapids: Wm. B. Eerdmans Publishing Company, 1984).

3. These categories are roughly those suggested by Nicholas Wolterstorff, "The AACS in the CRC," *The Reformed Journal* 24 (December 1974): 9-16.

4. Harry S. Stout, *The New England Soul: Preaching and Religious Culture in Colonial New England* (New York: Oxford University Press, forthcoming).

5. The Reformed efforts to build a Christian culture are well described in Fred J. Hood, *Reformed America: The Middle and Southern States, 1783-1837* (University, AL: University of Alabama Press, 1980).

6. Carl F. H. Henry, *The Uneasy Conscience of Modern Fundamentalism* (Grand Rapids: Wm. B. Eerdmans Publishing Company, 1947), 10.

7. See Robert Booth Fowler, *A New Engagement: Evangelical Political Thought, 1966-1976* (Grand Rapids: Wm. B. Eerdmans Publishing Company, 1982), for an account of this relationship and other developments in evangelical political thought.

1

THE DUTCH SCHOOLS

JAMES D. BRATT

Abraham Kuyper

In 1898 a Dutch Reformed minister recently arrived in the United States made his first contribution to that perennial topic of immigrant discussion, the contrast between Old World and New World cultures. For this observer, Foppe Ten Hoor, the difference appeared most clearly in work styles, which in turn reflected geographical constraints. In America, where land and resources existed in nearly absurd abundance, people who could work and move on quickly tended to stay on the surface of things, and regarded all affairs with pragmatic judgment. Netherlanders, however, with their limited terrain, had to be thorough and cautious, paying close heed to distinctions and boundaries, delving to the roots of things. The first group was enamored of results, action, and change; the second, with principle, theory, and tradition. The difference had consequences in all realms, Ten Hoor concluded, but most importantly in the theological.[1]

How his audience should negotiate the conflict that their mixed status (Dutch and American) entailed, Ten Hoor left to later occasions. More important for our purposes here is his delineation, on the verge of the twentieth century, of seminal "Dutch" characteristics; for the body of theological work the group would produce in that century bears out Ten Hoor's profile remarkably well. Most striking, perhaps, is Ten Hoor's very act of addressing such cultural concerns precisely in his role as professor of systematic theology at the Christian Reformed seminary in Grand Rapids. That the post brought with it this license, even mandate, to speak to any and all issues and that no office in the entire community held more prestige attest to the priority of place the Dutch Reformed have given theology.

Some of theology's function for this group is thus evident in Ten Hoor's decree. So is an uneasy duality at the heart of that function. On the one hand, as Ten Hoor insisted in hundreds of subsequent lectures and pages of commentary, Reformed doctrine was God's own truth, eternal, unchanging, fixed in his revelatory Word, the best interpretation of that Word. On the other hand, Dutch theology bore the stamp of a particular culture and was used by Ten Hoor and many others to differentiate "our people" from the "American world," even from other Reformed groups in that world. Quite simply, theology could not escape serving Dutch Americans as the medium of intellectual exchange, for their churches served as the center of their local communities and their denominations as the national networks binding these together. As all sorts of social dynamics and cultural issues—churchly or not, intraethnic or involving the outside world—registered in ecclesiastical terms, theology became the means of communal debate, confirmation, and resolution. Hence the theology professorship's broad portfolio and the community's doctrinal passion. Theology had to be but could not be left an eternal code of truth beyond the vagaries of interest and perception. Doctrine and life worked in a close and continuing dialectic, each speaking to the other as—and sometimes more—fully and directly as the fondest theorists of Calvinism might wish. Ten Hoor worked better than he knew in that quick, and quite typical, concluding leap from the earth to the religious.

Our analysis of this theology will move from the more common to the more particular; that is, first reviewing those elements that the Dutch share with other American Protestants, especially with evangelicals and other Reformed camps; then examining the features that have differentiated them from these; and finally tracing the issues of controversy within the community itself and the separate schools thereby produced. Put another way, we can describe Dutch-American distinctiveness and debates as functions of a particular selection and combination of elements from the general Reformed fund, and analyze that selection-combination process according to different trajectories of launch from the Netherlandic background, shifting patterns of consensus and tension within the community, and the ongoing dialectic between the community and the surrounding American world.

The Wider Context of Calvinism

The themes of commonality and particularity are prefigured in all three of Dutch Calvinism's confessional standards. That there were three suggests the motif of plurality as well. The Belgic Confession (1561), written in the fires of intense religious strife, gave primordial definition to the Dutch church, but also showed, in its anti-Catholic and anti-Anabaptist strains, how the Dutch could comport well with other Reformed movements whether on the continent or in America. The Heidelberg Catechism (1563), on the other hand, was famous for its pastoral, irenic nature. Written to promote unity between the Reformed and Lutherans in Germany, the document became as well a bridge between the Dutch and German Reformed, again on both sides of the Atlantic. Its practical piety also allowed its readers a way of negotiating the tension between orthodoxy and pietism that proved so disruptive elsewhere. Finally, the Canons of Dort (1619), forged in "a virtual ecumenical council of Reformed churches," buttressed the Dutch in their predestinarian, theocentric identity and in the scholastic methodology they would share for centuries with the descendants of Westminster.[2]

Since the proceedings at Dort coincided with the founding of New Netherland in the Hudson Valley, the Dutch church in North America came into being with this full confessional structure at its disposal. It hardly made distinguished use of this resource or of any other, however, subserving rather the colony's economic purposes and suffering with its demographic, political, and diplomatic misfortunes.[3] The English conquest (1664) cost the Dutch church its preferred status, and for the next century it remained in a mixed state—an enclave for ethnocultural maintenance, yet a base of significant public power, uneasily housing both Jersey farmers and a Manhattan commercial elite. These divisions were to some extent mirrored in the controversy that ensued upon New Jersey pastor Theodore J. Frelinghuysen's use of "awakening" measures in the 1720s.[4] By the 1750s the church had divided into two camps, the "Coetus" (representing the Frelinghuysen line, with a platform of pietism and home rule), and the "Conferentie" (New York-based, holding more to the Amsterdam connection and confessional-liturgical traditions). Each group established connections with the respective "New" and "Old Light" factions in denominations around them. Yet rather than gravitating to these other orbits, the two sides were reunited with each other in the 1770s. The architect of the fusion, John H. Livingston, aptly represented the church's settled character: pious and intellectual, American (Yale) and Amsterdam educated, in contact with outsiders but first attentive to the home front.[5]

Signal features of this process, it should be noted, were no more "distinctively American" than characteristically "Dutch Reformed." The Netherlands was as central in the rise of evangelical pietism as pietism was in that nation's religious history in the century after 1650. Frelinghuysen himself was a child of the movement and brought it with him as an immigrant to America in 1720.[6] Moreover, in the Dutch case pietism generally had confessional orthodoxy as an ally, not—as often happened elsewhere—as an antagonist. This was the result of the long struggle within the Netherlandic church between the followers of Jacobus Arminius (and later, Descartes) and the strict Dortian party, which saw the former gradually gain tolerance, then dominance, so that orthodoxy became a minority view among the church elite. Over the same period, the more devout in hundreds of local congregations had been organizing conventicles to help prosecute a more rigorous type of religion than the established church could enforce. These found the themes of orthodoxy quite more to their taste than liberal esteem of reason and human nature; and the traditionalist theologians found in them a welcome base of support.[7] It was here, then, that pietism and confessionalism were married; that Gijsbert Voetius, champion of orthodoxy, and Willem à Brakel, exemplar of practical divinity, were bound together, to be venerated for generations as chief of "de oude schrijvers," "fathers" of the true faith.[8]

Such loyalties also figured prominently in the two developments of early nineteenth-century Dutch history most germane to our purposes. In the post-Napoleonic restructuring of the Reformed Church, local autonomy seemed threatened by an increasingly centralized administration, which had—even worse—opened the way for liturgical and doctrinal "corruption." The ensuing "secession" (in 1834) and formation of a network of "truly Reformed" churches essentially represented the old conventicle principles and clientele in more radical guise.[9] A decade later, the Seceder network provided key mechanisms of mobilization, transportation, and leadership for a new wave of Dutch emigration to America. Since this precedent was remembered for the whole second phase (1845-1920) of Dutch immigration, and since emigration and Secession appealed to the same strata of Dutch society, the orthodox made up a disproportionately high percentage of the nineteenth-century immigrants—and of the post-World War II migrants to Canada as well.[10] Hence the conservative branches of Dutch Calvinism took a central role in shaping the new ethnic subculture.

A pietist-confessionalist conjunction in the conventicle-Seceder mode thus forms the baseline of Dutch theology in America. It was also the source of the group's several similarities with its new Protestant neighbors. Like every strain in the American revivalist-evangelical tradition, Dutch pietism insisted that faith be deep, personal, and heartfelt, that it proceed from and through a bare confrontation with one's own unworthiness and the exclusive merits of Christ. Postconversion, the believer was to maintain the intimacy of this deliverance through daily introspection and devotions; was to "practice godliness," rejecting the "things of the flesh and the world"; and throughout, was to submit to the appraisal, admonition, and encouragement of the fellow "faithful."[11] Doctrinal comparisons, on the other hand, are more difficult since American evangelicals have hardly been of one mind on theological detail. But the Dutch have shared their characteristic, unifying insistence on a high view of scriptural veracity and authority, on Christianity's finality, and, in face of Enlightenment and Modernist critiques, on the plausibility and necessity of the supernatural, miraculous, and transcendent in religion and metaphysics. As one of their typical assessments concluded, the Fundamentalist "is our fellow believer," but the Modernist "is on the side of the anti-Christ and cannot be recognized as a believer at all."[12] So were the Dutch placed on the American spectrum.

The full extent of these congruences was best evident in the 1925-1950 era. Both the Dutch and the evangelicals entered the period lashed by the cultural crisis that had been precipitated by World War I. Both responded with a subcultural strategy—the Dutch reinforcing an inherited structure, the evangelicals building theirs new. Both took militant anti-Modernism as their overriding outlook, their prime motive force, for the entire era; and both moved toward strict, maximal claims as a result. On the side of ethics, the era began for the Dutch with their largest denomination officially (and unprecedentedly) proscribing three forms of "worldliness": dancing, gambling, and theater attendance.[13] An evangelical's list might have looked somewhat different (usually including smoking and drinking, which were still tolerated—if no longer virtually mandatory—among the Dutch), but the strategy of defensiveness, legalism, and symbolic repudiation of larger cultural trends was the same. As to theology, this was the clearest era of confessionalist hegemony in Dutch-American history. Appropriately, Louis Berkhof was its presiding figure; his *Reformed Dogmatics,* in three volumes, its definitive production. Though it became the best-known Dutch contribution to American theology, Berkhof's work had first of all an intracommunal intent. It was to be at once the *summa* of the inherited faith and the touchstone for measuring all other (read, "outside") opinion, an intellectual fortress amid "the widespread doctrinal indifference . . . superficiality and confusion . . . [and] insidious errors" of "the present day." Yet virtually any evangelical of the era, even those put off by Berkhof's Reformed insistencies, could cheer the priority (in logic, deference, and elaboration) he gave to Scripture, and relish his emphatic reassertion of every doctrinal construction offensive to liberalism.[14]

Dutch Distinctives

The very degree of similarity, however, prompted demonstrations of particularity. Not only did Berkhof's anti-Arminian strictures have this role vis-à-vis most revivalist and holiness movements; so did the confessional thoroughness and intensity, the systematization and doctrinalism evident in the Dutch tradition. If Berkhof's statement of purpose intended "insidious errors" for Modernists, "widespread doctrinal indifference, superficiality and confusion" covered large reaches of the evangelical complex. It was there (to conclude Berkhof's statement) that "sects . . . are springing up like mushrooms on every side." Nor was this Berkhof's complaint alone. From his predecessor, Foppe Ten Hoor, to his successors in the post-World War II era, from every Dutch-American denomination, from press as well as pulpit, the Dutch mounted a persistent critique of American Protestantism's creedal reductionism, and of the cultural spirit it evidenced. From this perspective, Fundamentalism with its "short list" and Modernism with its "no list" of "essential doctrines" looked oddly similar, and the "Bible alone" claims of small sects only echoed the doctrinal ignorance of big denominations. The phenomenon in general showed that the churches were mirroring all too faithfully the character of the society around them. The individualistic egotism and pragmatism of the second appeared as the characteristic "subjectivism" and "moralism" of the first—that is, the designation of personal experience or feelings on the one hand or practical action on the other as *the* core, and inevitably the extent, of Christianity.[15]

Confessional consciousness, expectably, offered several corrective counterpoints. For Foppe Ten Hoor, it presented a foil against Anglo-American—and not coincidentally, Arminian, subbiblical—ways.[16] For the more optimistic, it opened up the treasures, and the warning lessons, of the centuries of church history.

> To turn one's back on the historic creeds is therefore to turn one's back on what God has given us through the struggle of centuries, and to run the risk of trying to build up once more what has already been tried and found wanting. . . . To preach a creed is one of the very best methods possible . . . of avoiding tangents and vagaries, of securing a balanced and full-orbed presentation of the Bible as a whole. . . .[17]

But for everyone, it forestalled the drift to liberalism on the left and pious self-absorption on the right to which the subjective impulse was particularly prone. The confessions alone had the resources equal to the challenges and temptations of modern culture. Moreover, this seemed the scripturally given psychology. True, one must experience salvation and prove it in action; but without recourse to the full body of biblical truth, to a holistic system mindful of first principles and aware of their logical implications and complications, these would prove fleeting, filled more with the spirit of the age than with that of the Word.[18]

Besides doctrinalism, several specific tenets worked to distinguish the Dutch among conservative Protestants. Persistently, discussions in this vein brought up the ideas of covenant and kingdom. The intertwining of the two and the vision they supported were best articulated by Abraham Kuyper (1837-1920), the eminent Netherlander whose Neo-Calvinistic movement did much to restore the concepts to the heart of Dutch

Reformed concern.[19] Of the dual goals that drove Kuyper throughout his staggeringly multifarious career, success in the first—combatting liberalism—required the second—awakening the devout from their pietistic slumbers. To be *Calvinists* again, Kuyper told his followers, they had to recognize the lordship of Christ over all areas of life, which meant that they could neither dismiss various fields (art, science, politics) as inherently "worldly" nor participate in these simply with and as non-Christians, but must bring into each a distinctively Christian commitment and program. The result would be an "organic church," working outside ecclesiastical institutional walls, but with a coherent plan and mutual discipline, living out the Word of God in "every sphere of life" and so building up the Kingdom of God in the midst of the world. Covenant figured centrally in this conception as the mechanism or ground of divine sovereignty (the "channel through which the waters of election flow"), just as kingdom denoted its scope or end.[20]

One measure of the Kuyperian presence among Dutch-Americans, their perennial efforts at Christian cultural action, has been much noted. It was from Kuyper that they got their early concern with "worldview," their habitual confidence in speaking to every phase of modern culture, from science to social theory, geopolitics to economics, and their determination to uncover philosophical preconceptions in every academic credo, every social program. But the covenant-kingdom conjunction itself played a major role in this project by shaping a Dutch-American church ethos that contrasted markedly, in their eyes, with that of the evangelical world. Put simply, covenant was arrayed against revivalism as a model of Christian initiation and against dispensationalism as a view of history; and kingdom stood over against individualism as the scope of God's purpose, and against mere soul-saving as the end. Against spiritual moods, the pressures of life, and faddish "winds of doctrine," the covenant rooted the believer firmly in social and historical context, and above all in the lasting will of God. He did not exist as a lonely individual but as part of a corporate body that supported him even as he contributed to its vitality. He did not have to extract the full message of faith from the Bible anew, nor alone puzzle out its complicated relationships with daily life, for he stood heir to the whole heritage of Christian history. Nor was the present era a parenthesis in the divine plan, allowing of only "spiritual" ends and means for Christian action. God's ages were an organic whole, as were his people, so a full-bodied, earthly witness to redemption was still the Christian mandate. Drawing off lifelong nurture, not just a single episode (periodically "renewed") of emotional "conversion," the life of faith would not be restricted to Sunday worship and special "spiritual" moments during the week but would involve everyday habits, customs, and work in home, shop, and school. More boldly, placed in the fabric of his peers and the order of generations past and present, believers could transcend the level of personal ethics alone and address collective structures, broad cultural movements, with the redemptive message.[21]

This vision manifests the basic axioms of Dutch Reformed thinking: the will of God, not the whims of man; organic connections, not fragments or individual parts. But the program's usual implementation shows the ethnic-communal factor in the group's life as well. "Kingdom-building" was too readily left at the construction of a cradle-to-grave institutional framework for the mutual association of Dutch-Americans; and the magisterial process of divine election through the corridors of time could devolve to just the baptism and indoctrination of the group's next generation. "God does not save people at random," said one commentator to this point, "but follows a certain order, and perpetuates his covenant from generation to generation through the families of believers"—Dutch-American believers, it turned out.[22] Grand visions and small achievements thus became the besetting paradox of this group. But perhaps that only manifested the dissonance it felt in the new land. With so few sharing their tastes, they worried with considerable realism that their salt liberally sprinkled might only lose its savor.

The "outsiders" with whom the Dutch felt most compatible were the "old Princeton" sector of American Presbyterianism. Confessionalism, theocentricity, and some of the same cultural vision the two shared. Just as important were the personal links between them: Geerhardus Vos, West Michigan's donation to the Princeton Seminary faculty in 1893, who drew a generation of future Dutch Reformed leaders there for graduate training; and J. Gresham Machen, who popularized the conservative Presbyterian cause among the Dutch in the great battles of the 1920s, winning funds and faculty for his new institutions.[23] But even here affinities were crossed by differences, the most obvious being epistemological. First, Princeton theology, deeply beholden to Scottish Common Sense Realism, tended to minimize the effect of sin upon human reason. Second, it posited that Christianity—and Christianity alone—was a rationally demonstrable and coherent system, that any fair-minded person could and would see the same and be brought to faith accordingly, and that apologetics was therefore the theologian's highest labor. Dutch Neo-Calvinism, in contrast, joined continental dialectical Idealism to a radical Augustinian psychology. There simply was no religiously neutral rational faculty or middle ground, Kuyper insisted again and again. Reason, like every other faculty, impulse, or activity, proceeded from and worked to serve one's fundamental commitment—in Kuyperian parlance, one's (necessarily religious) "life-principle." Accordingly, the world could contain any number of relatively coherent worldviews, none of which could finally convince another of its own superiority on strictly rational grounds. Apologetics would therefore be the last concern of the theologian, who should work instead to elaborate the full complex of faith on its own presuppositions for the battle of world systems.[24]

This disagreement hardly broke relations between the two schools. Benjamin B. Warfield, the lion of Princeton, praised Kuyper's work even though this part of it "utterly mystified" him.[25] But especially with J. Gresham Machen, Warfield's successor, further variances were shown that, added to the first, subtly complicated the connection. Machen's reformation of culture aimed at "all areas of thought," Kuyper's at "all areas of life." Machen had an individualistic, contractarian, and laissez-faire view of the state and society (and the first two also for the church), all of which were anathema to Kuyper. Kuyper's approach was intuitive, passionate, and populistic; Machen's intellectualist, controlled, aristocratic.

Though Machen differed with Kuyper in significant ways, he brought to the faculty of Westminster Theological Seminary a disciple of Kuyper's, Cornelius Van Til. Kuyper had discerned an absolute antithesis in all of life (including all scholarly work) between believer and unbeliever. The consequences of the Fall is a radically abnormal world. Only the sovereign regenerating work of the Holy Spirit can overcome the rebellion of unbelief. Van Til used Kuyper's notion of the antithesis to develop his presuppositional apologetics. For Van Til unregenerate man actively suppresses his knowledge of God. Man is not ignorant, he is rebellious. Man is never neutral or objective in his evaluation of evidence. Rather, in every act of interpretation and understanding man acts either as a servant of God or as an unbeliever asserting his autonomy. A key task of apologetics is to show the inadequacies of non-Christian or inconsistently Christian thought. This perspective led Van Til to analyze not only what a theologian or philosopher said, but also what he should have said according to the basic orientation of his views. Van Til pressed people to face the necessary extension of their views. After Machen died, Van Til's apologetic system gained the enthusiastic support of the Westminster faculty.

Machen's orthodox Presbyterians, nonetheless, did not converge as steadily with the Dutch Reformed as might have been expected. The principal theological divergence over time involved the issue of biblical infallibility. The Kuyperian stress on the inner testimony of the Holy Spirit allowed an alternative to the Princetonian inerrancist-propositional model. Only some among the Dutch Reformed (and those the more identifiably Kuyperian, though Van Til was not among them) took that option, however; their opponents (perhaps the more traditionally confessional) preferred the more Princetonian conception. It might have been only appropriate, in turn, that the Presbyterian-based Rogers-McKim proposal showed considerable debts to Dutch Calvinist sources.[26]

Conflict Within Dutch Faith

This hint of intracommunal differences brings us to our third area of concern, the persistent presence of conflict within the Dutch Reformed circle itself. The most striking instance was its early division into two denominational camps: the Reformed Church in America (RCA), descended from the colonial era and attracting the early leadership and much of the rank and file of the post-1845 immigration; and the Christian Reformed Church (CRC), which emerged out of two breaks with that leadership, one in 1857, the other in 1880, and eventually garnered a majority of the later arrivals.[27] The CRC also inherited, therefore, virtually all of the Kuyperian influx into Dutch America and all of the tensions with the Seceder school that Neo-Calvinism induced. Thus, pietist-confessionalist vs. Neo-Calvinist is the second strain persisting throughout the group's history. Finally, both of these parties could divide within themselves as well, and forge coalitions across their earlier opposition. Thus, sometimes Kuyperians stood together against the pietists; other times some Kuyperians and pietists joined together against other kinds of Kuyperians and pietists; and throughout, the two denominations engaged each other variously in open warfare, armed peace, or cool suspicion.

The denominational divide did not simply reflect, as was long surmised, the Seceder–National Church rivalry from the Old World. The immigrant (Western) sector of the RCA and the CRC were equally beholden at their origins to Seceder clergy and clientele. Rather, the schism grew out of a tension within the Secession itself, which allowed two different perceptions of the Reformed heritage and the American situation. The RCA West represented that wing of the movement oriented toward experiential piety and practical morality—the very emphases, of course, of the antebellum American evangelicalism in which the RCA East participated. The affinity was reinforced by the correspondence between evangelicalism's favored-church status in the nineteenth century and the increasingly National Church background of the immigrants the RCA West attracted after 1880.[28] Thus the RCA became fixed on the relatively conservative side of mainstream Protestantism: generally orthodox but not overly concerned with Reformed confessional specifics; convinced of the Protestant character of the United States, and enthusiastic for the various early twentieth-century crusades designed to strengthen that character at home and spread it abroad. That stance persisted even after the crusades had failed. The RCA maintained in the post-Protestant ethos of mid-twentieth-century America the distinguishing marks of a mainstream affiliation: membership in the National and World Councils of Churches, wariness of anti-Modernist crusading, and entertainment of proposals for church union.[29]

That each of these was challenged from within the RCA West shows, however, the persistence there as well of the more cautious, confessionally emphatic Secessionist stream. That tradition was even stronger—we might say predominant—in the CRC, characterizing Ten Hoor and Berkhof on the seminary level and the majority of the denomination's clerical and editorial leaders through at least World War II. To this perspective, modern times constituted not an opportunity but a threat for faith, and the church was called not to move into the world but to attend to the loyal remnant. America's "Christian character" turned out to be a seductive veneer hiding a secular heart; and maximal Reformed consciousness—rather than ecumenical ventures in either the revivalist or social reform mode—seemed the only antidote sufficient to the threat. Yet befitting their common Seceder rootage, this was a defensive, as the RCA optimists' was an outgoing, pietism. Neither countenanced Kuyper's holistic, systemic approaches; both focused their energies within the institutional church, upon individual soul-saving and personal behavioral symbolics—we might say, upon missions and moralism.[30]

Neo-Calvinist discontent with this posture flared both in pointed disputes and in a persistent culturalist concern. The latter was clearly evident, for example, in the 1930-1950 era of Confessionalist hegemony when certain CRC ministers and academics, clustered around Calvin College and Seminary, sponsored conferences and a monthly journal dedicated to providing a comprehensive and distinctively Reformed interpretation of current philosophical, sociopolitical, and international affairs. Only such, this party claimed, was adequate to both the richness of the Christian heritage and the desperate needs of the modern era. Yet this project's anti-Modernist agenda comported well enough with the Confessionalists' to keep peace in the denominational house.[31] Such harmony did not always obtain. In fact, both the earliest and the latest theological battles in the CRC grew from the pietist–Neo-Calvinist tension, and both involved questions arising from that traditional seedbed of Reformed controversy, the doctrine of predestination.

In the first dispute (1890-1905), the timing of election itself opened the issue. The supralapsarians, representing the Neo-Calvinist line, placed election before the fall of man, indeed before creation itself, and correlatively placed regeneration virtually at birth, before baptism and "conversion experiences," which were taken as merely confirming what had already been effected by the will of God. This construction, the supras argued, best fit Calvinism's theocentricity, anchored the individual's salvation in the eternal will of God, and released the pulpit and pew from emotionalism and self-absorption for the comprehensive cultural witness that was the church's true business. The infralapsarians' reversals on all these points bespoke their Seceder heritage. So did their critique of the opposition's clientele. Abstract speculation might please the "dreaming philosophers," the arrogant elite, that comprised Kuyper's movement, Foppe Ten Hoor declared, but the health of the Reformed churches would lie always with the humble, who cherished the vital piety that Scripture and confession had ever mandated. Let "scientific" theologians have their worldly glory; the despised of the earth would inherit the Kingdom of Heaven. Happily for Ten Hoor, the infras' success in this case did not have to wait that long, as the Synod of Utrecht's (1905) decision for their side of the debate was accepted in Dutch America as well.[32]

The most recent controversy in the CRC involved similar hostilities but quickly moved from the nature of the will of God to the nature of his Word. Again the intelligentsia precipitated the conflict (in 1962), only this time arguing that election, as expressed in the Dortian statement on limited atonement, could be read as unduly restrictive. The Confessionalists saw this as an attack upon their hegemony, and the CRC Synod's somewhat tepid resolution of the matter in 1967 proved them right.[33] For the two sides almost immediately (1969-1972) clashed again over a more momentous issue, the nature and authority of Scripture. With this debate, denominational control shifted to the "progressives" who stood, albeit at some remove, in Kuyper's descent. The Confessionalists' inerrant-propositionalist constructs were demoted, though hardly excised, at crucial points. The Bible's authority, the Synod declared, lay not simply in divine inspiration but in its redemptive message; its meaning and veracity involved not so much empirical "facts" in various domains (geological, biological, historical) as its purpose of salvation and its focus in Christ.[34] A more clearly Neo-Calvinist formulation also entered the field at this juncture, reflecting the influence of Herman Dooyeweerd, one of Kuyper's successors at Amsterdam, among post-World War II immigrants to Canada. The Dooyeweerdians, as they became known, articulated a tripartite notion of revelation: besides (and perhaps through and before) the Inscripturated (Bible) and Incarnate (Christ) Word stood God's creation ordinances (the Law Word), by which the Christians' redemptive witness to all areas of society and culture could proceed. The Confessionalists could hardly decide which of these constructions troubled them more, and could draw little comfort from the rivalry between the two.[35] Indeed, one reason for the 1970s change in denominational power was the alliance of the two Neo-Calvinist parties, as opposed to the mutual recrimination and then coalescence, by one side or the other, with the Confessionalists that had occurred at two earlier crises.

That Kuyper spawned two schools instead of one owed largely to a basic ambiguity in his thought. On the one hand, Kuyper preached religious antithesis: the life-principles of Christians and unbelievers were diametrically opposed, the spiritual qualities of their respective actions were inevitably antagonistic, and Christians should therefore pursue their work in society from their own separate organizations. Later in his career, without diminishing this idea, Kuyper resurrected the doctrine of common grace: that God gave to humanity grace which, while not "saving," enabled them to attain much virtue and truth; that achievements in politics and scholarship, art and technology, which were not motivated by faith might still be cherished as gifts of God; and that cooperation between Christians and unbelievers was therefore possible and necessary.[36] Kuyper's American followers, unable to harness this paradox as had their master, diverged into schools that can be designated antithetical and positive. The first saw corruption (in principle and practice) present everywhere in the world, stressed the negative or condemnatory purpose of Christian sociocultural witness, and absolutized the need for separate organization. The second hoped to realize some of the improvements that the Christian critique offered society and sanctioned cooperation with people of different principles to this end.[37] That the Kuyperians thus divided along the same defensive-outgoing lines as had the pietists explains the types of interparty coalitions that were made. That the two fiercest conflicts in CRC history occurred between the two Calvinist factions, and both times in the wake of world wars, demonstrates the group's metaphorical use of theology. Common grace, as the doctrine relating the church to the world, cast in theological terms the question of Dutch America's relation to the outside world, exactly the issue that wartime nationalism had raised most intensely.

The first of these battles, like that of the early 1970s, took rise from the issue of Scripture. Drawing connections with the Modernist-Fundamentalist debate then reaching its zenith, a Confessionalist-Antithetical coalition in the early 1920s accused Roelof Janssen, chief positive Calvinist on the Grand Rapids faculty, of practicing higher criticism in his Old Testament instruction and of thereby partaking dangerously of the rationalistic and naturalistic spirit of the age. Janssen's reply, however appealed to Kuyper, Herman Bavinck, and other Reformed authorities, continental and American, to establish his orthodoxy and to turn the charges back on his critics. It was their denial of common grace, explicit among the Antitheticals, implicit among the Confessionalists, Janssen argued, that forced them to denigrate humanity's residual abilities, to eliminate God's grace from the natural realm, and to misconstrue the nature of miracles, revelation, and science. The debate's increasing focus on the relations between Old Testament Israel and surrounding nations hinted at the cultural issue involved: both sides saw the future of the Dutch "Israel" in America to be at stake. Enough of the community were suspicious of "progressive" adaptation to the nation that had, in World War I, so badly treated them that the tide swung against Janssen. He guaranteed the conclusion by refusing to testify before the 1922

Synod.[38] But then the tide swung against the Antithetical members of his prosecution, the CRC pastors Herman Hoeksema and Henry Danhof. Their absolutizing of the antithesis, and post-facto declaration that common grace had indeed been the root issue in the Janssen case, cost them their Confessionalist allies. These coalesced with positive Calvinists at the 1924 Synod to declare Hoeksema and Danhof in error. Common grace was Reformed orthodoxy, though more useful for evangelism than for cultural cooperation, and Hoeksema and Danhof were ordered to stop saying otherwise. They did not, and joined Janssen in the ranks of the demoted.[39]

The Confessionalist regime that this settlement installed lasted until after World War II. Then the drama was played out again, only with a less conclusive ending. Again, a "progressive" party arose at Calvin Seminary (George Stob and Harry Boer, with James Daane helping from the outside), eager to bear positive witness to the American world. Again, the Confessionalist majority brought accusations of the "heresy" currently in the air, i.e., "Barthianism"; and again they allied with Antithetical voices—Cornelius Van Til and H. Evan Runner—to quash the new school. The battle at the Seminary was dismissed (also the fate of the entire faculty) as a conflict of personalities, however, and the factions settled into uneasy coexistence.[40] Antitheticalism came to lodge chiefly among the Canadians in the CRC, positive Calvinism in the *Reformed Journal* and the denominational bureaucracy, and intelligentsia Confessionalism in *Torch and Trumpet* (later the *Outlook*), northwest Iowa, and assorted clergy who felt increasingly displaced, marginalized, in their own denomination.

Future Prospects

What will be the future course of Dutch-American theology depends much upon the future course of the community it has guided and served. Here signs are ambiguous. As to factional differentiation, each party now has connections with natural allies in the American Protestant world: the Confessionalists with conservative Presbyterians, Lutherans, and other battlers for the Bible; both types of Kuyperians with "progressive" elements in neo-evangelicalism; the RCA West with mainstream sociopolitical missions in the World Council of Churches. But each group has also returned to Netherlandic models for sustenance: Dort, Dooyeweerd, G. C. Berkouwer, and A. A. van Ruler, respectively.[41] As to communal persistence, the group's theological productivity has never been so high; neither, thanks to televised religion, has its rank and file ever been so open to non-Reformed pieties, programs, and personalities of every sort. As to past issues of debate, common grace—

because it was so tied to the question of acculturation—will not likely cause uproar again, although its implications will be detectable. The question of hermeneutics will probably remain central, although less in itself than because of the clashing sociocultural agendas for which it has been both source and legitimation. The outcome of that struggle, finally, lies hidden in the oldest subject of dispute, the will of God, which for these Calvinists must always be the beginning of the matter, and the end.

Notes: The Dutch Schools

1. Foppe M. Ten Hoor, "De Amerikanisatie onzer Kerk," *Gereformeerde Amerikaan* 2 (May-June 1898): 180-87, 206-15. See similarly (all in *Gereformeerde Amerikaan*) his "Het Engelsch Christendom," 5 (October 1901): 457-63; "Is het Christendom in Strijd met de Rede?" 18 (March 1914): 106-20; and a second series on Americanization, 13 (January-March, May, September 1909).

2. For the background of these documents, see Philip Schaff, ed., *The Creeds of Christendom* (New York: Harper, 1877), 1:502-23, 531-54. The quoted phrase is from Sydney E. Ahlstrom, *A Religious History of the American People* (New Haven: Yale University Press, 1972), 203.

3. For a capsule survey, see Ahlstrom, *Religious History*, 200-204; George L. Smith, *Religion and Trade in New Netherland* (Ithaca: Cornell University Press, 1973), is a detailed study.

4. The best biography is James Tanis, *Dutch Calvinistic Pietism in the Middle Colonies: A Study of the Life and Theology of Theodorus Jacobus Frelinghuysen* (The Hague: Martinus Nijhoff, 1967). See also Herman Harmelink III, "Another Look at Frelinghuysen and His 'Awakening,' " *Church History* 55 (1968): 423-38.

5. These events are presented in close detail in John P. Luidens, "The Americanization of the Dutch Reformed Church" (Ph.D. diss., University of Oklahoma, 1969).

6. Tanis, *Dutch Calvinistic Pietism*, 16-41.

7. F. Ernest Stoeffler, *The Rise of Evangelical Pietism* (Leiden: E. J. Brill, 1967), 116-17, 127-48.

8. On Brakel, ibid., 156-57; on Voetius, see Otto de Jong in A. G. Weiler et al., *Geschiedenis van der Kerk in Nederland* (Utrecht: Aula, 1963), 138-40. Dutch parishioners in America were reading these authorities in the pulpit and in private as final arbiters as late as 1900; see Henry Beets, *De Christelijke Gereformeerde Kerk in Noord Amerika* (Grand Rapids: Grand Rapids Printing Company, 1918), 22-27.

9. The best recent treatment of the Secession in Dutch is H. Algra, *Het Wonder van de 19e Eeuw* (Franeker: T. Wever, 1966). See also James D. Bratt, *Dutch Calvinism in Modern America: A History of a Conservative Subculture* (Grand Rapids: Wm. B. Eerdmans Publishing Company, 1984), 5-10.

10. The relevant data and bibliography on this much discussed issue are available in ibid., 7-10, 227-28. Hereafter, "Dutch" and "Dutch Reformed" have reference to the ethnoreligious community in North America, unless otherwise indicated.

11. Stoeffler gives great detail on the Dutch case vis-à-vis general pietist contours in his *Rise of Evangelical Pietism*, 109-79 and 6-23, respectively.

12. Clarence Bouma, "Ecumenism: Spurious and Genuine," *Calvin Forum* 15 (November 1949): 61-62. For the sources and contours of Dutch theological antiliberalism, see Bratt, *Dutch Calvinism*, 20-22, 127-31, 134.

13. See *Agenda of the Synod of the Christian Reformed Church, 1928*, 4-56.

14. Louis Berkhof, *Manual of Reformed Doctrine* (Grand Rapids: Wm. B. Eerdmans Publishing Company, 1933), 5; this was the one-volume distillation of *Reformed Dogmatics* (Grand Rapids: Wm. B. Eerdmans Publishing Company, 1932), intended for more popular use. For Berkhof's treatment of Scripture, see *Reformed Dogmatics*, 1:14-18, 24-30, 138-79. His broader critique of liberalism is evident in *Aspects of Liberalism* (Grand Rapids: Wm. B. Eerdmans Publishing Company, 1951).

15. Pre-World War I analyses of this sort, directed at "Methodism," are covered in Bratt, *Dutch Calvinism*, 58-60, 248-49; and Henry Zwaanstra, *Reformed Thought and Experience in a New World: A Study of the Christian Reformed Church and Its American Environment, 1890-1918* (Kampen: J. H. Kok, 1973), 43-49. For the interwar commentary, see Bratt, *Dutch Calvinism*, 132-34, 273-75.

16. Foppe M. Ten Hoor, "Het Engelsch Christendom," *Gereformeerde Amerikaan* 5 (October 1901): 457-63, and "Is het Christendom in Strijd met de Rede?" *Gereformeerde Amerikaan* 18 (March 1914): 106-20.

17. John E. Kuizenga, "Why We Need a Creed," *Leader*, 22 November 1922, 9.

18. Of very many statements on this point, a few succinct declarations are Clarence Bouma, "How Dead Is Calvinism?" *Calvin Forum* 1 (October 1935): 51-52; Ralph Stob, "Men of Principle," *Banner*, 29 November 1935, 1086; Lewis Smedes, "Evangelicals, What Next?" *Reformed Journal* 19 (November 1969): 4. Exemplary larger works are Bastian Kruithof, *The Christ of the Cosmic Road* (Grand Rapids: Wm. B. Eerdmans Publishing Company, 1937); and Henry Zylstra, *Testament of Vision* (Grand Rapids: Wm. B. Eerdmans Publishing Company, 1956).

19. A fine, brief introduction to Kuyper in English is Dirk Jellema, "Abraham Kuyper's Attack on Liberalism," *Review of Politics* 19 (October 1957): 472-85; see also Bratt, *Dutch Calvinism*, 14-33. An excellent sketch in Dutch is Jan Romein, "Abraham Kuyper: De Klokkenist der Kleine Luyden," in *Erflaters van onze Beschaving* (Amsterdam: Querido, 1971). Three representative works of Kuyper in English translation are *Lectures on Calvinism* (Grand Rapids: Wm. B. Eerdmans Publishing Company, 1961 [1898]), *Christianity and the Class Struggle* (Grand Rapids: Piet Hein, 1950 [1891]), and *To Be Near Unto God* (Grand Rapids: Wm. B. Eerdmans Publishing Company, 1924).

20. See J. C. Rullman's precis of Kuyper's fullest elaboration of the doctrine of the covenant (*De Leer der Verbonden* [Amsterdam, 1885]), in *Kuyper-Bibliographie* (Kampen: J. H. Kok, 1940), 3:251.

21. This material is more fully elaborated in James D. Bratt, "The Covenant Traditions of Dutch Americans," in Daniel Elazar and John Kincaid, eds., *The Covenant Connection: Federal Theology and the Origins of Modern Politics* (Carolina Academic Press, forthcoming). Primary works from three different eras are John Van Lonkhuyzen, *Heilig Zaad* (Grand Rapids: n.p., 1916), 3; William Hendriksen, *The Covenant of Grace* (Grand Rapids: Wm. B. Eerdmans Publishing Company, 1932), 12-13; and Andrew Kuyvenhoven, *Partnership: A Study of the Covenant* (Grand Rapids: Board of Publications, CRC, 1974). Secondary analyses of these themes are conveniently available in Peter De Klerk and Richard R. De Ridder,

eds., *Perspectives on the Christian Reformed Church* (Grand Rapids: Baker Book House, 1983): Anthony A. Hoekema, "The Christian Reformed Church and the Covenant," 185-201; and Fred H. Klooster, "The Kingdom of God in the History of the Christian Reformed Church," 203-24.

22. Hendriksen, *Covenant of Grace*, 65.

23. Bratt, *Dutch Calvinism*, 107, 128-29. Names and statistics of CRC leaders attending "old Princeton" are available on p. 270, n. 21. Dutch-related members of the Westminster Seminary faculty were R. B. Kuiper, Ned B. Stonehouse, and Cornelius Van Til.

24. George M. Marsden, *Fundamentalism and American Culture: The Shaping of Twentieth Century Evangelicalism, 1870-1925* (New York: Oxford University Press, 1980), 114-16, gives a succinct comparison. Much greater detail, from the Kuyperian point of view, is available in John Vander Stelt, *Philosophy and Scripture: A Study in Old Princeton and Westminster Theology* (Marlton, NJ: Mack Publishing Company, 1978).

25. Marsden, *Fundamentalism and American Culture*, 115.

26. Jack B. Rogers and Donald K. McKim, *The Authority and Interpretation of the Bible: An Historical Approach* (New York: Harper and Row, 1979); the Dutch theologians concerned are Gerrit C. Berkouwer and, through him, Herman Bavinck, Kuyper's contemporary in Amsterdam. A critical assessment of this connection is Richard B. Gaffin, Jr., "Old Amsterdam and Inerrancy?" *Westminster Theological Journal* 44 (1982): 250-89, and 45 (1983): 219-72.

27. A review from the RCA side is William Van Eyck, *Landmarks of the Reformed Fathers* (Grand Rapids: Wm. B. Eerdmans Publishing Company, 1922); from the CRC side, Henry Beets, *De Christelijke Gereformeerde Kerk in Noord Amerika*, 66-120. Valuable statistical and social scientific analyses of the first schism are available in Robert P. Swierenga, "Local-Cosmopolitan Theory and Immigrant Religion: The Social Bases of the Antebellum Dutch Reformed Schism," *Journal of Social History* 14 (Fall 1980): 113-35, esp. 123.

28. Swierenga, "Local-Cosmopolitan Theory," 123, 130.

29. Herman Harmelink III, *Ecumenism and the Reformed Church* (Grand Rapids: Wm. B. Eerdmans Publishing Company, 1968), illustrates, directly and indirectly, all three of these points.

30. This mentality in the CRC is presented in great detail for the 1890-1918 era in Zwaanstra, *Reformed Thought and Experience*, 70-95; over the longer run in Bratt, *Dutch Calvinism*, 47-50, 125-41, 190-95, 207-10. On the RCA side, ibid., 125, 135-37, 197-99, 205-06.

31. The journal was the *Calvin Forum*; for its views, see Bratt, *Dutch Calvinism*, 126, 142-56.

32. Ibid., 46-49. Exemplary statements on the infra side are Foppe M. Ten Hoor, "Principieele Bezwaren," *Gereformeerde Amerikaan* 9 (May and August 1905); Lammert J. Hulst and Gerrit K. Hemkes, *Oud- en Nieuwe-Calvinisme* (Grand Rapids: Eerdmans-Sevensma, 1913). On the supra side, John Van Lonkhuyzen, *Heilig Zaad*, and Richard Gaffin, ed., *Redemptive History and Biblical Interpretation: The Shorter Writings of Geerhardus Vos*, 231ff., 240-47, 263ff.

33. On this, the so-called "Dekker" case (after its protagonist, Harold Dekker, Professor of Missions at Calvin Seminary), see Dekker's articles in the *Reformed Journal*, December 1962-March 1963, and those of James Daane and Harry Boer in the same periodical, October 1964-March 1965. The opposition's case was best made by R. B. Kuiper in *God-Centered Evangelism* (Grand Rapids: Baker

Book House, 1957), and "Professor Dekker on God's Universal Love," *Torch and Trumpet* 13 (March 1963): 4-9. For the Synodical debate, see *Acts of Synod of the CRC, 1967,* 486-607, 727-38.

34. For the final statement, known as "Report 44," see *Acts of Synod of the CRC, 1972,* 493-546.

35. This principle and its implications are dramatically presented in John A. Olthuis et al., *Out of Concern for the Church* (Toronto: Wedge Publishing Company, 1970). The Confessionalist response is John Vander Ploeg, "One 'Word of God' or Three?" *Outlook* 22 (February 1972): 5-8.

36. Bratt, *Dutch Calvinism,* 18-20; Simon J. Ridderbos, *De Theologische-Cultuurbeschouwing van Abraham Kuyper* (Kampen: J. H. Kok, 1947), 30-131, 233-57.

37. Bratt, *Dutch Calvinism,* 50-54; Zwaanstra, *Reformed Thought and Experience,* 95-131.

38. Bratt, *Dutch Calvinism,* 105-10, presents a review of the case and its literature.

39. Ibid., 110-15. Whereas Janssen went into exile as a broker in Chicago, Hoeksema and Danhof started their own denomination, the Protestant Reformed Church.

40. Ibid., 190-96. The principals' major statements on the issue were: Cornelius Van Til, *Common Grace* (Philadelphia: Presbyterian and Reformed Publishing Company, 1947); H. Evan Runner, "Het Roer Om!" *Torch and Trumpet* 3 (April 1953): 1-4, and a series in the same journal, April-October 1955; William Masselink, *General Revelation and Common Grace* (Grand Rapids: Wm. B. Eerdmans Publishing Company, 1953); and James Daane, *A Theology of Grace* (Grand Rapids: Wm. B. Eerdmans Publishing Company, 1954).

To put all these debates in chronological order:
1) RCA-CRC split, 1857 and 1880-1882.
2) Supra-Infra debate, 1890-1905.
3) Common grace I (Janssen and Hoeksema cases), 1918-1924.
4) Common grace II, 1950-1960.
5) "Dekker case" (limited atonement), 1962-1967; leading on to "Report 44" debate (nature and authority of Scripture), 1969-1972.

41. On the role of Dooyeweerd and Berkouwer, see nn. 35 and 26 above, respectively. On the example of Dort, see, e.g., Peter Y. De Jong, ed., *Crisis in the Reformed Churches: Essays in Commemoration of the Great Synod of Dort, 1618-1619* (Grand Rapids: Reformed Fellowship, 1968). On A. A. van Ruler, see the special issue of *Reformed Review* devoted to him: 26 (Winter 1973).

2

LOUIS BERKHOF

HENRY ZWAANSTRA

Louis Berkhof

DURING the period prior to the First World War, the Christian Reformed Church was self-consciously and openly Dutch-American. As hyphenated Americans, members and leaders in the Christian Reformed Church were preoccupied with Americanization. Being deeply committed to their Dutch Reformed theological and churchly heritage, they strenuously sought to resist the intrusion of American religious ideas and practices that would detract from or otherwise endanger their inherited tradition. Yet they were Americans convinced that they had a special task and calling in America. Louis Berkhof belonged to this generation. He was thoroughly bilingual, capable of expressing himself with equal facility in either Dutch or English. He was also deeply committed to preserving the Dutch Reformed theological tradition in the Christian Reformed Church. This tradition, properly preserved and represented, he believed was relevant for American thought and life.

Early in the twentieth century, the climate of theological opinion in America was not particularly conducive to dogmatic theology nor cordial to historic Reformed theology and Calvinism. The intellectual spirit of the age promoted the rise and progress of liberal theology and the Social Gospel. At the same time it provoked a conservative reaction that took the form of Fundamentalism. Louis Berkhof did his theological reflection and work in this environment. Before he concluded his career, Neoorthodoxy or Crisis Theology appeared on the American scene. He interacted with this theology, too, in its initial stages.

Louis Berkhof's life and work were immersed in the Christian Reformed Church. To it he devoted his time and energy. He served the Christian Reformed Church briefly as a pastor and preacher. For 38 years he was a professor of theology. During the last 13 of these years, he was also the president of Calvin Theological Seminary. He regularly served as an advisor to Christian Reformed Church synods. Being a gifted public speaker, Berkhof frequently addressed convocations and audiences.

It was, however, as a writer that he made his greatest and most enduring contribution to the Christian Reformed Church.

Being a person with broad interests, Berkhof wrote on many subjects. In addition to the theological works for which he is best known, he addressed social issues and problems, modern trends of thought, and such matters as Christian education, evangelism, missions, and the spiritual life. He was a contributor to periodicals widely read within the Christian Reformed Church such as *De Gereformeerde Amerikaan* (The Reformed American) and the *Calvin Forum*. He also regularly wrote series of articles in the denominational weeklies, *The Banner* and *De Wachter*. Berkhof's impact on the American theological world and the theological world at large was an uncalculated and unanticipated result of the favorable reception of his publications in systematic theology.

Formative Years: 1873-1906

Louis Berkhof was born on October 13, 1873, in Emmen, Drenthe, The Netherlands. His parents, Jan and Geesje (ter Poorten) Berkhof, were members of the Christelijke Gereformeerde Kerk (Christian Reformed Church). This church came into existence as a result of a secession from the Nederlands Hervormde Kerk (Netherlands Reformed Church) or state church in 1834. The Berkhofs' religious life, like that of most members of the churches of the Secession of 1834, consisted of deep and simple piety fused with devotion to the Reformed faith articulated in the historic confessions of the Reformed churches in The Netherlands. In 1882, when Louis was 8 years old, the Berkhof family emigrated to the United States, settling in Grand Rapids, Michigan.

At this time the Neo-Calvinist movement in The Netherlands under the leadership of Dr. Abraham Kuyper was already well underway. Kuyper was a man of extraordinary genius and deep personal piety. In addition to leading a second secession from The Netherlands Reformed Church in 1886 called the "Doleantie," Kuyper was the founder of the Free University of Amsterdam (1880) and its first professor in dogmatics. He was instrumental in bringing into existence a Christian school system from the elementary to the university level. He greatly advanced the cause of separate Christian labor organizations and succeeded in making the Anti-Revolutionary political party founded by Groen van Prinsterer into an effective Christian political force. For many years Kuyper served in the Dutch Parliament and was twice elected Prime Minister. The churches of the secessions of 1834 and 1886 united in 1892 to form De Gereformeerde Kerken in Nederland (The Reformed Churches in The Netherlands). The Neo-Calvinist movement, the Kuyperian ideas that inspired it, and the impact it made on social, political, and church life in The Netherlands all exercised considerable formative influence on the Christian Reformed Church in America and on the life and thought of Louis Berkhof.

When Louis was a teenager, he was an active member (secretary) of the first Reformed Young Men's Society organized in Grand Rapids, Michigan.[1] The society's purpose was to study Reformed doctrine and the principles of Calvinism for all areas of human life. Later Berkhof was reported to have said that he owed more to the young men's society than he would ever be able to repay. In that society he learned to study and express himself. There he also began to realize that God had given him some talents for labor in his kingdom. And there, he said, the desire to serve God in the ministry was awakened and began to ripen.[2] Berkhof was one of the first to urge the local society to organize on a denominational scale. The American Federation of Reformed Young Men's Societies soon came into existence. For many years Berkhof's book, *Subjects and Outlines*, specially prepared for the American Federation in 1918, was used as a study guide. The work covered a wide range of subjects: Bible History, Reformed Doctrine, General and American Church History, and various educational, social, and political issues. It concluded with a long list of resolutions for debate. After becoming a theological professor, Berkhof continued to show his loyalty to the organization and to repay the debt he owed to it by serving no less than 15 years on its Executive Board.[3]

Sometime in 1893 Berkhof publicly professed his faith in Christ in the Alpine Avenue Christian Reformed Church. In September of that year at the age of 19, he enrolled in the Theological School of the Christian Reformed Church. At the time the Theological School consisted of two parts, a literary department with a four-year course of study and a theological department with a three-year program of study. The literary department was gradually expanded into Calvin College and the theological department later became Calvin Theological Seminary.

In the spring of 1893 the Theological School sustained a severe loss when the youthful, brilliant, and much-loved professor of dogmatics and exegetical theology, Geerhardus Vos, accepted an appointment to teach biblical theology at Princeton Seminary.[4] Vos did, however, leave his reputation and unpublished lectures in dogmatics behind. Berkhof heard about the former; the latter he undoubtedly used.

Hendericus Beuker was Berkhof's teacher in dogmatics. Beuker was a graduate of the Theological School of the Christelijke Gereformeerde Kerk in Kampen, The Netherlands. After distinguishing himself as a capable pastor and churchman in The Netherlands, he emigrated to America in 1893. The following year he was appointed to teach dogmatics. Beuker's intellectual gifts were certainly adequate to the task. He was a severe critic of the German liberal theology and higher criticism of the day. Although himself an infralapsarian, he respected Kuyper for his scholarly work and appreciated the counterforce Kuyper posed to the "fearfully destructive hurricanes" coming out of the German universities.[5] Beuker was most favorably impressed with the theological thought and erudition of Herman Bavinck. When the first volume of Bavinck's *Gereformeerde Dogmatiek* (Reformed Dogmatics) appeared, Beuker judged it a fundamental contribution to theological science and a great blessing for the Reformed churches.[6] Early in 1900, the same year Berkhof graduated from the Theological School, Beuker died. Foppe M. Ten Hoor began teaching dogmatics in the fall of that year and continued to do so until retirement in 1924.

On September 16, 1900, Louis Berkhof was ordained to the ministry in the Christian Reformed Church in Allendale, Michigan. Less than two years later, his name was included in a list of potential candidates for appointment to a new chair in exegetical theology. The appointment, however, went to Roelof Janssen, a relatively unknown quantity in the Christian Reformed Church except for the fact that he held a Ph.D. degree from the University of Halle in Germany and was studying at Kampen. Janssen's advanced degree, even though it was not in theology, influenced the outcome of the synod's decision.[7] Berkhof decided to seek more formal education.

From 1902 to 1904 Berkhof studied at Princeton Seminary, a bastion of Reformed orthodoxy. There he came under the tutelage of Benjamin Warfield and Geerhardus Vos. Both men were staunch defenders of Reformed confessional orthodoxy and the authority of Holy Scripture, including verbal infallibility and inerrancy. H. Henry Meeter, professor of Bible at Calvin College and for many years a close personal friend of Berkhof, reported that Berkhof frequently said that he owed more to Vos than anyone else for his insights into Reformed theology.[8] Princeton awarded Berkhof the Bachelor of Divinity degree.

In August 1904, Berkhof was installed as minister of the Oakdale Park Christian Reformed Church in Grand Rapids, Michigan. There he quickly established a reputation for his insights into Scripture, carefully crafted sermons, and gifts in public speaking.[9] In addition to his work in the congregation, Berkhof promoted the cause of Christian education in the denomination with a pamphlet published in 1905, *Het Christelijk Onderwijs en Onze Kerkelijke Toekomst* (Christian Education and the Future of Our Church). While at Oakdale Park he also took some courses, chiefly in philosophy, by correspondence through the University of Chicago.

The Board of Trustees did not recommend Janssen for reappointment in 1906. Unresolved conflicts had arisen between him and Ten Hoor regarding the authority of the church in the study of theology. Furthermore, some members of the board were convinced that Janssen's teaching unmistakably leaned toward higher criticism. [10] In the absence of a recommendation from the board, the synod prepared a nomination for exegetical theology. Berkhof, the vice president of the synod, was included in the nomination and later chosen by a large majority to fill the vacant chair. [11]

Professor of Exegetical Theology and New Testament Studies: 1906-1924

On September 5, 1906, in the Commerce Street Christian Reformed Church, Louis Berkhof was installed as professor of exegetical theology. The same evening he delivered an inaugural address in the Dutch language entitled "De Verklaring der Heilige Schrift" (The Exposition of the Holy Scriptures). It was a noteworthy occasion and address. Berkhof argued that the correct interpretation of Scripture was contingent on a proper understanding of the Scriptures' peculiar character as the Word of God. He then proceeded to indicate how Scripture itself was threatened by many dangers such as higher criticism, liberal theology, modern biblical theology, and recent historical and archaeological discoveries. He concluded by emphasizing the great importance of the view of Scripture and its interpretation that he presented for ministers of the Word. [12]

From 1906 to 1914 Berkhof taught all the Old Testament and New Testament courses offered at Calvin Seminary: Hebrew, New Testament Greek, Old Testament and New Testament Exegesis, Introduction to the Old Testament and New Testament, and Old Testament and New Testament History.

In 1911 he published in the Dutch language a textbook on biblical hermeneutics. [13] In comparison with recent hermeneutical studies, Berkhof's treatment was simple and unsophisticated. In a manner that was to become characteristic of Berkhof, he first dealt with the task and history of the science of biblical interpretation, and then elaborated the essentials of the grammatical-historical theological method. In 1937, this work, only slightly edited, was published for the use of English-speaking students under the title *Principles of Biblical Interpretation*. During the time Berkhof taught both Old and New Testament he published only one special study, a pamphlet on the book of Joshua, *Life Under the Law in a Pure Theocracy* (1914).

In spite of his heavy teaching load and the breadth of his assignment, Berkhof did not neglect the pressing social issues and problems agitating the American church world and the Christian Reformed Church. For the benefit of the Dutch-American members of the Christian Reformed Church, Berkhof wrote *Christendom en Level* (Christianity and Life). As the title suggests, the work dealt with a wide range of issues pertaining to Christianity and culture. It also specifically addressed needs confronting Reformed people of Dutch ancestry as they faced the American world. Published in 1912, the book was described in *De Wachter* as one in which lines were drawn, fundamentals laid out, and valuable counsel given.[14]

The following year Berkhof wrote *The Church and Social Problems*. This was his first English-language publication. The pamphlet better than any other single source illustrates the breadth of Berkhof's interests and sympathies, his knowledge of contemporary American theological literature, his capacity for balanced judgment, and his ability to engage discursively and critically in theological issues and problems. In this work Berkhof gives a strikingly different impression from that presented in his textbooks on theology.

Berkhof proceeded on the assumption that the gospel of Jesus Christ was the greatest liberating force in the world, eminently applicable to the pressing social problems of the age. After briefly outlining the nature of the present social problem including quotations without additional critical comment from such works as Walter Rauschenbusch's *Christianity and the Social Crisis* and Josiah Strong's *The Challenge of the City*, Berkhof surveyed the history of the church's role in the existing social crisis. He acknowledged that the church itself contributed to the crisis and that many of the charges being brought against the church for social negligence, such as aiming at the salvation of the individual only while showing little concern for the regeneration of society, and preaching a one-sided "other-worldly" gospel that did not touch the realities of life, were true. The church definitely had social duties and responsibilities that were not being met.[15]

Berkhof thought the church, both as a spiritual fellowship of believers and as an organization, had a task in the movement for social reform. Natural and spiritual life could not be neatly compartmentalized, nor could the responsibilities for human life simply be parceled out so that the church as an institution found its duty only in the spiritual sphere. The church as an organization also had a role to play in social reforms. After emphasizing that the church should be a nursery for true, healthy, and vigorous spiritual life, Berkhof forthrightly asserted that the church should never forget the social message entrusted to it. The church was God's chosen instrument not only to save individuals and to prepare them for eternal life, but also to implement as much as possible the Kingdom of God on earth. The Bible contained many directives for social life, revealed principles that should control social reform, and offered the only final solution to social problems. Ministers of the gospel should fearlessly and clearly proclaim the broad principles underlying social life. The church also should exemplify in its own social life the social principles for which it stood in addition to bringing the gospel to the masses in the great cities of the nation. The church, he said, ought to make a thorough study of the present social problems and of the various movements working for social improvement. In conclusion Berkhof sounded the separatistic note characteristic of many Kuyperian Calvinists calling Christians to organize on a distinctively and positively Christian basis for social and philanthropic action.[16]

In 1914 the synod decided to divide exegetical theology into Old Testament and New Testament departments. Berkhof was given the assignment in New Testament. In spite of previous difficulties with Roelof Janssen, the synod by a sizable majority elected him to teach Old Testament.[17]

A reduced teaching load and a more narrowly circumscribed area of research enabled Berkhof to put his pen to work. In 1915 he wrote *Biblical Archaeology*, a study in the history and cultures of the Ancient Near East, and *Introduction to the New Testament*. *The Christian Laborer in the Industrial Struggle* appeared the following year. Although this pamphlet exhibited the same learned qualities as his earlier address on social issues, its focus was more limited and its purpose more parochial. Berkhof wrote to persuade the Christian Reformed Church of the incompatibility of membership in religiously neutral labor organizations and membership in the church of Christ.[18]

In the midst of the international turmoil and upheavals occasioned by the First World War, Henry Bultema, pastor of the First Christian Reformed Church in Muskegon, Michigan, published *Maranatha*.[19] The central thesis of Bultema's book was that the unfulfilled prophecies in the Bible should be interpreted literally just like those that have already been fulfilled. Bultema also attempted to defend chiliastic and premillennial views. *Maranatha* provoked an immediate response in the Christian Reformed Church. Berkhof was asked to speak on the subject. He did so in English. At the request of friends and because of the urgency of the matter, Berkhof had his address published in edited and expanded form in Dutch.[20] In April 1918 *Premillennialisme: Zijn Schrifttuurliche Basis en Enkele van Zijn Practische Gevolgtrekkingen* (Premillennialism: Its Scriptural Basis and Some of Its Practical Consequences) appeared. Berkhof cordially and judiciously refrained from mentioning Bultema in the text. In the notes Bultema and *Maranatha* appear along with other American premillennialists and their works.

After expressing great respect for the premillennialists' unconditional acceptance of the Bible as the Word of God and for the warmth of their devotion to Scripture, a striking contrast to the "icebergs of higher criticism," Berkhof proceeded to elaborate four objections to their views. Berkhof's first and most fundamental objection was to the premillennialists' mistaken insistence on a strictly literal interpretation of the prophetic writings. According to Berkhof the historic Christian church in its exegesis of prophecy self-consciously accepted and applied a different hermeneutical principle from that of the premillennialists. Those holding premillennial views did not deal adequately with the progressive and historical character of God's revelation. Berkhof insisted that the historical form in which a prophecy was given belonged to the essence of the prophecy and that it was proper to make a distinction between a literal historical explanation of a prophecy and its fulfillment. Berkhof also criticized the premillennialists for not interpreting Scripture according to the analogy of Scripture. In this respect they were following a practice wholly in agreement with modern, liberal exegetes. Berkhof further stated that Revelation 20:4-6 should also be interpreted according to the analogy of the New Testament. The Dutch theologians Kuyper, Bavinck, Greydanus, and Hoekstra so interpreted the text, as did Warfield, Vos, Milligan, and Eckman. And finally Berkhof asserted that by insisting on a literal fulfillment of prophecy the premillennialists got involved in all kinds of contradictions and bound God in fulfilling prophecies to conditions and situations that existed when the predictions were first given.[21]

Berkhof's second objection to premillennialism focused on the thousand-year kingdom of Christ and the doctrine of the second resurrection. After a rather extensive treatment of the texts appealed to in support of the doctrines, Berkhof concluded that the scriptural basis for both was very weak.[22]

Thirdly, Berkhof objected to the premillennialists' absolute separation of Israel and the church. The separation resulted in a denial of the spiritual unity between them. Berkhof argued that this separation and denial destroyed the unity of God's revelation, conflicted with the organic nature of his redemptive work, negated the salvation of humanity in Jesus Christ, and robbed the church of Christ of the blessings of the covenant.[23]

Finally, Berkhof objected to the premillennialists' customary use of the distinction between the Kingdom and the church in the New Testament. Again they separated the two so that Christ's present kingship was denied. Quoting Vos, Berkhof argued that the church is a form that the Kingdom takes after Christ's death and resurrection. He concluded by saying that the Kingdom is a present reality, its subjects are united with Christ in the church, and Christ is now really king.[24]

The synod agreed with Berkhof. Bultema and *Maranatha* were tested strictly by the standards of Reformed confessional orthodoxy and found wanting for separating Israel and the church, and the church and the

Kingdom, thus denying the spiritual unity between Israel and the church and the present kingship of Christ. Bultema was later deposed. He and his followers formed the Berean Church.[25]

In 1919 Louis Berkhof and three of his colleagues, William Heyns, Foppe Ten Hoor, and Samuel Volbeda, sent a letter to the Board of Trustees informing the board that student reactions to Janssen's teaching "irresistibly" raised the question whether or not Janssen was doing an injustice to the authority, infallibility, and trustworthiness of Holy Scripture.[26] The four professors did this without previously talking to Janssen. A bitter and heated controversy resulted. On the basis of student notes the four professors contended that Janssen denied the Mosaic authorship of the Pentateuch, the historicity of miracles recorded in the Bible, and the messianic significance of certain passages of the Old Testament. Janssen's explanation of many other Old Testament passages was also objectionable.[27] In the professors' judgment the Reformed doctrine of the inspiration, authority, infallibility, and trustworthiness of Scripture was threatened.[28] Given the rationalistic principles undergirding Janssen's approach, the professors predicted that his teaching, if allowed to continue, would certainly lead to a surrender of the authority of Scripture to modern critical science and a denial of Scripture as a divine redemptive revelation. It would also rob members of Christian Reformed congregations of their infallible rule for faith and life and the denomination of its Reformed distinctiveness, causing it to sink away into the watered-down Christianity so evident in the American world.[29]

Janssen replied to the four professors. In his reply he stated that all science including theology has for its aim the discovery of truth. In the quest for truth the empirical approach could not be avoided; thus all theological investigation, in the nature of the case, had to be critical. Janssen further affirmed that his scientific work rested on the presupposition that Scripture was God's infallible revelation. Nevertheless, in interpreting Scripture Scripture itself should be allowed to speak. The interpreter should not allow his presuppositions to determine the meaning of the text. Scripture stood above dogmatics and the latter should not be permitted to control the former. The meaning of Scripture, therefore, should not be a foregone conclusion. According to Janssen the Dutch Reformed theologians Kuyper, Bavinck, Aalders, and Grosheide agreed with this position.[30]

Janssen refused to appear at the synod where the matter was to be adjudicated because many of his accusers were also delegated to synod and in his judgment it was unfair for them to operate at the same time as plaintiffs and judges.[31] On the basis of the student notes, the synod found Janssen's point of view and method deficient because he did not give faith the role it deserved in theological science and because he did not allow the Bible as the divinely inspired Word of God to predetermine his conclusions. The synod also criticized him for subjectifying special revelation. Although the synod was careful not to charge Janssen with denying the inspiration of Scripture, it said that elements in his teaching could not be harmonized with the Reformed understanding of inspiration. The synod deposed Janssen from office.[32] Since Janssen had no following in the church, a schism did not result. A few younger ministers did, however, leave the church due to their unhappiness with the synodical procedures and the deposition.[33]

During the years of the Janssen controversy, Louis Berkhof's reputation as a theologian and churchman accelerated both inside and outside the Christian Reformed Church. In 1919 Berkhof was offered the presidency of Calvin College.[34] Three years later he was asked to become the editor of *De Wachter*.[35] Berkhof declined both appointments. During the 1920-21 academic year, Berkhof was invited to give the Stone Lectures at Princeton Seminary. He spoke on "The Kingdom of God in Modern Thought and Life."

In 1924 the Christian Reformed Church was again embroiled in theological controversy. The issue this time was common grace. Two capable and popular ministers, Herman Hoeksema and Henry Danhof, had written and spoken against the doctrine. Berkhof did not get directly involved in the dispute before the meeting of synod. In adjudicating the matter the synod officially declared three points: (1) the existence of a general or common grace of God shown to all men, (2) the restraint of sin by the general work of the Holy Spirit, and (3) the ability of the unregenerate to perform civic righteousness.[36] Disciplinary measures against the ministers who opposed the doctrine of common grace and the synodical decisions led to a schism of some proportion and to the formation of the Protestant Reformed Church. The following year, when protests and appeals were still pending, Berkhof entered the controversy with *De Drie Punten in Alle Deelen Gereformeerd* (The Three Points in All Parts Reformed). In 1926 the synod did not sustain the protests and appeals of the opponents of the three points.

Professor of Systematic Theology and President of Calvin Seminary: 1926-1944

After teaching dogmatics in the Dutch language for 24 years, Foppe Ten Hoor retired in 1924. Although the synod considered shifting Berkhof from New Testament studies to dogmatics, it decided instead to appoint Dr. Clarence Bouma as professor of dogmatics.[37] Two years later, the synod decided to separate apologetics and ethics from dogmatics. Bouma chose the former areas of theology, thus creating a vacancy in the latter. That Berkhof aspired to teach dogmatics was common knowledge in the church.[38] In the judgment of some his work on the "Three Points" clearly demonstrated an ability to do so.[39] Berkhof's interest went beyond a simple personal predilection. He considered biblical studies in some respects preparatory to the science of dogmatics, which made use of the fruits of biblical theology.[40] The synod complied with many interests and desires and appointed Louis Berkhof professor of dogmatic theology.[41]

After 1926 the turbulent storms of theological controversy in the Christian Reformed Church subsided never to return again with the same intensity during Berkhof's lifetime. The church had purged itself of premillennialism, the threat of free scientific inquiry and biblical criticism, and the danger of too narrow a conception of the operation of the Holy Spirit in human cultural life. With the retirement of Ten Hoor, the last vestige of enthusiastic infralapsarianism also disappeared.[42] An amazing theological consensus, basically conservative and deeply rooted in traditional Reformed confessional orthodoxy, resulted. In this general climate of theological opinion, and in harmony with it, Berkhof engaged in theological research, reflection, teaching, and writing.

During the first years that he taught dogmatics, Berkhof concentrated on research and teaching. He produced a special doctrinal study, *The Assurance of Faith*, in 1928. In 1931 the Board of Trustees decided to discontinue the annual rotating Rectorship at Calvin Seminary and to appoint a more permanent administrative head. Berkhof was a logical choice. He had frequently functioned as the spokesman for the faculty and had during the present academic year served very capably as Rector. Moreover, he enjoyed the confidence of the church and the respect of the students. The board elected Louis Berkhof the first President of Calvin Seminary, a position he held concomitantly with his professorship for 13 years.[43]

On September 9, 1931, a celebration was held commemorating Berkhof's 25th anniversary as professor of theology. On the same festive occasion he was installed as president of Calvin Seminary. Berkhof delivered an inaugural address entitled "Our Seminary and the Modern Spirit." The address is noteworthy in that it clearly indicated the content and direction of his thinking. In the speech Berkhof also commented on the specific purpose and task of Calvin Seminary. He began by putting the subject in historical perspective. During the previous century the modern scientific method and the theological thought of Schleiermacher made an impact on theological education. The Social Gospel also produced an increased emphasis on applied Christianity. As a result of these new directions seminaries were now breaking away from church control, and, under the banner of intellectual freedom, were loosing themselves

from the authority of God's Word. A clearly discernible shift from dogmatics to practical theology and from church-centered to social-centered
interests was also évident. Berkhof said that Calvin Seminary had not
adapted itself in the past to these new directions and that it would not
in the future accommodate itself to any changes that would compromise
its stand on the Word of God and on the confessional standards of the
church. Calvin Seminary did not recognize erring human reason as a
source of divine truth and would not permit it to stand in judgment on
the Word of God. The seminary would continue to honor the supernatural and would refuse to submit to present-day liberalism, which was
bound to degenerate into pure naturalism. Speaking in the first person
Berkhof said, "We accept the Reformed system of truth which was handed
down to us by previous generations, attempt to exhibit it in all its com-
prehensiveness and in all its beauty and logical consistency, seek to
defend it against all opposing systems, and endeavor to carry it forward
to still greater perfection in harmony with the structural lines that were
clearly indicated in its past development."[44]

As a professor of systematic theology, Berkhof believed his primary
task was to present scriptural truth comprehensively and in logical order
and to do so in a manner compatible with historical Reformed theology.
He further sought to illuminate Reformed thought by contrasting it with
what he considered aberrant doctrinal positions. In treating a doctrine,
Berkhof ordinarily defined and presented the Reformed view, commented briefly on the history of the doctrine, then indicated the scriptural basis for the Reformed position, and finally discussed and critiqued
alternative views. His basic criticism of Roman Catholic theology was
that it made the hierarchical church the source of and authority for dogma.
His sharpest barbs were, however, directed at modern liberal theology.
This school of thought reduced theology to anthropology or to the mere
study of religion. In Berkhof's judgment the modern psychological, so-
ciological, and philosophical approaches to religion could never satisfy
the demands for genuine theological inquiry and statement. Wherever
appropriate he summarized and commented critically on the theologies
of Schleiermacher and Ritschl. Berkhof's treatment of contemporary
neoorthodoxy and neoorthodox theologians such as Barth, Brunner, and
Niebuhr was brief, but not without penetrating insight. He appreciated
their criticism of modern liberalism, their consciousness of the broken
human condition, and their emphasis on the necessity of special revelation and the grace of God for salvation. He did not, however, agree
with their basic theological position, and the strictures they placed on
Reformation theology. Consequently he sincerely doubted that their
thought represented historic Calvinism.[45]

According to Berkhof the object of investigation in theology was the knowledge of God as he revealed himself in Holy Scripture. Although it is impossible for man to know God as God knows himself, God could be known because and insofar as he revealed himself. In a somewhat Hegelian manner, Berkhof asserted that the knowledge of God formed the content of special revelation. Special revelation itself was an unfolding of the knowledge of God and the redemptive idea in Christ Jesus.[46] Although strictly speaking special revelation was broader than Holy Scripture, practically and concretely special revelation was synonymous with Scripture. Consequently Holy Scripture was the sole source for the subject matter of dogmatic theology. It was also the only authoritative norm or standard for judging the truth formulated and affirmed in theology.[47]

In Berkhof's judgment Reformed systematic theology was a scientific enterprise.[48] Holy Scripture contained truths in the form of facts and ideas, but it did not present a logical system that could simply be copied. The Bible, however, did itself suggest that the truths it presented were interrelated. God also saw truth as a unit and the truth revealed in the Word of God was an organic whole. Moreover, man as a rational creature had an irrepressible urge to comprehend truth in its unity. The peculiar task, therefore, of the systematic theologian was to think God's thoughts after him under the guidance of the Holy Spirit, to assimilate comprehensively the truth revealed in the Word of God, and to reproduce it logically in systematic form. Although Berkhof strenuously rejected the use of speculative reason as a source and norm of theological truth, he affirmed the proper and necessary function of reason for uniting the particular ideas and facts contained in the Word of God and for organizing them into a coherent system of truth. Reason should not, however, be permitted to function independently of faith. In theological science faith corresponded with the revealed knowledge of God and served as the necessary instrument within man for appropriating divine truth. In brief, faith appropriated revealed truth, reason organized and systematized it.[49]

And finally, according to Berkhof, Reformed dogmatic theology was an ecclesiastical affair. The church as a whole under the guidance of the Holy Spirit engages in the reflective activity that produces dogma. When the church collectively reflects on the truth of God's Word, this truth takes definite shape in the consciousness of the church and is formulated in clearly defined doctrines. Although Scripture always remains the source, norm, and final test for all dogmatic truth, the creeds and confessions of the church provide a nucleus of subject matter for dogmatic theology. Berkhof insisted that the theologian is always the theologian of a particular church. He receives the truth in the fellowship of the church, shares the church's convictions regarding it, and promises to teach in harmony with it as long as the church's understanding of the truth is not contrary to the Word of God.[50]

A surprising number of systematic theologians met Berkhof's basic criteria. He approved the works of the American theologians Robert Breckinridge, James H. Thornwell, Robert L. Dabney, Charles Hodge, Archibald A. Hodge, William G. Shedd, Henry B. Smith, Benjamin B. Warfield, and John L. Giradeau. He much preferred, however, the writings of the Dutch Reformed theologians Kuyper and Bavinck.[51]

Berkhof's major writings in systematic theology grew out of his classroom work and as textbooks were intended to meet the needs of students who could no longer read Kuyper and Bavinck. His *magnum opus*, *Systematic Theology*, was first published in two volumes in 1932 with the title *Reformed Dogmatics*. Later the same year the *Introductory Volume to Reformed Dogmatics* appeared in print. A revised and enlarged edition of *Reformed Dogmatics* was published in one volume in 1941 with the title *Systematic Theology*. Again, Berkhof revised the introductory volume and, in order to bring it in line with the major work, he renamed it *Introductory Volume to Systematic Theology*. Berkhof did not make a case for the change in titles except to say that it seemed better in America to use the title "Systematic Theology." He also called attention to the fact that even Warfield had defended the title.[52] To complete the textbook series in systematic theology, Berkhof in 1937 wrote a brief but comprehensive *History of Christian Doctrines*. Berkhof's book indicates that he was acquainted with a large body of literature on the subject including the works of Harnack, Loofs, Seeberg, and Newman. In it he descriptively presented the history of Christian doctrine in an orderly, nonjudgmental way. To assist students in their study of systematic theology, Berkhof's *Textual Aid to Systematic Theology* was published in 1942. In addition to these textbooks Berkhof wrote two special doctrinal studies, *The Vicarious Atonement through Christ* (1936) and *Recent Trends in Theology* (1944), before he retired.

Louis Berkhof was not a creative and imaginative theologian. Although he recognized that the systematic theologian had a critical as well as a constructive and defensive task,[53] he was not reflectively critical of the system he proposed nor aware of serious theological problems yet to be resolved. He believed that Reformed theology since Calvin had through the centuries assumed a more or less definite form.

In the Preface to his *Introductory Volume* published in 1932, Berkhof acknowledged that the general plan of his work was based on the first volume of Bavinck's *Gereformeerde Dogmatiek* and that in a few chapters he followed Bavinck's argumentation as well. In the revised edition, Berkhof included no such admission. Except for later additions, especially comments on neoorthodox theologians whom Bavinck antedated,

Berkhof, however, remained dependent on Bavinck for both the structure and content of his theology. In his *Systematic Theology*, Berkhof was only slightly less dependent on Bavinck. In this work Berkhof often re-arranged materials taken from Bavinck's volumes and occasionally introduced a new division of the material. Berkhof's treatment of Barth and Brunner in the 1941 edition was original work. Nevertheless Berkhof's theology was essentially the theology of Herman Bavinck. Berkhof was also dependent on Bavinck for the names of most of the theologians he mentioned and on whose views he commented. The scriptural references Berkhof cited were for the most part taken from Bavinck's volumes. Bavinck, however, usually referred to many more texts than Berkhof, and occasionally Berkhof cited passages not found in Bavinck. Berkhof was, however, pervasively dependent on Bavinck, often to the point of literally reproducing Bavinck's words and phrases.[54]

Louis Berkhof possessed remarkable intellectual and personal gifts for doing systematic theology. A voracious reader and diligent scholar, Berkhof was theologically well informed. He had a unique capacity to assimilate a large body of material, to sort out its essential content, and reproduce it in condensed form. He was especially adept at defining theological terms and making theological distinctions. His clear, concise, coherent, and systematic lectures and writings bore the stamp of his penetrating and orderly mind. As a person he was reserved, dignified, gracious, humble, and thoroughly human. Berkhof was no fighter. He innately disliked controversy. These intellectual gifts and personal qualities combined in Berkhof to produce a theologian who knew how to present Reformed doctrine in a systematic way and who could at the same time accurately represent and fairly judge other theological positions.

Berkhof retired in 1944. At the time he retired, he was still physically and mentally vigorous. He later wrote *Aspects of Liberalism* (1951), *The Kingdom of God* (1951),[55] and *The Second Coming of Christ* (1953). When he died on May 18, 1957, he was still regularly contributing articles in the church periodicals on Christian doctrine.

No theologian or churchman has made a greater impact on the Christian Reformed Church than Professor Berkhof. During the 38 years of his professional career, he was directly involved in the instruction and training of over 300 Christian Reformed Church ministers. His textbooks in systematic theology became virtual standards of Reformed theological orthodoxy in the Christian Reformed Church. For many years candidates for the ministry were examined by the synod before being declared eligible for the ministry. In these examinations each candidate was questioned for twenty minutes on the introduction (prolegomena) to Reformed theology and for another twenty minutes on each of the six loci of systematic theology. After sustaining the synodical examination, a candidate had to submit to a similar examination in systematic theology at the classical level before being ordained to the ministry. In these examinations Berkhof's *Systematic Theology* provided both the basis for the questions and the content for the correct answers.

Reports on the celebrations honoring Berkhof when he became president of Calvin Seminary and when he retired as well as memorial articles that appeared in the church papers when he died indicate that he was greatly esteemed as a person and scholar and much trusted as a teacher and churchman. No one else in the history of the Christian Reformed Church has been so honored and respected.

Berkhof established a theological reputation in America almost exclusively through the publication of *Systematic Theology*. An Eerdmans' advertisement stated that since the death of Warfield, Hodge, Kuyper, and Bavinck, Professor Louis Berkhof occupied a unique place in the world of Reformed dogmatics. His *Systematic Theology* was unequalled by any contemporary treatise in the English language. The advertisement further quoted Samuel G. Craig, who said that Berkhof's work was the most important work on systematic theology from an American source to appear in recent years.[56] In addition to Calvin Seminary many other conservative American theological schools and Bible colleges have used Berkhof's *Systematic Theology* as a textbook for instruction.[57]

Berkhof's *Systematic Theology* brought him international recognition as a Reformed theologian. English editions of his work have been sold in Australia, Canada, South Africa, England, and other European countries. This work has also been translated into Chinese, Japanese, Korean, Spanish, and Portuguese.

Recognizing Berkhof's administrative experience and his international reputation as an orthodox Reformed theologian, the delegates from conservative Reformed churches from many parts of the world chose Louis Berkhof to be the president of the first assembly of the Reformed Ecumenical Synod meeting in June 1946 in Grand Rapids, Michigan.

Notes: Louis Berkhof

1. *Young Calvinist*, October 1931, 3.
2. *Young Calvinist*, July 1957, 4.
3. Ibid.
4. Geerhardus Vos graduated from the Theological School in 1883. The same year Vos enrolled in a postgraduate course of studies at Princeton Seminary. From Princeton he went to the University of Berlin where he studied for one year. In 1888 Vos received a Ph.D. degree from the University of Strassburg. From 1888 to 1893 he taught at the Theological School where his work was highly

esteemed by his colleagues and students. Although no criticism was expressed regarding his teaching in biblical studies, opposition was raised to his dependence on Kuyper, especially Kuyper's supralapsarianism, in dogmatics. Vos's decision to go to Princeton was based on a variety of things, not the least of which was the attractiveness and challenge of the Princeton offer. The new chair of biblical theology at Princeton was very likely specially designed to offset the influence of Dr. Charles A. Briggs, who taught the same subject at Union Seminary in New York. Vos's first love was biblical theology, not dogmatics.

5. Address to the Synod of the Reformed Churches in The Netherlands in 1899, printed in *Acta der Synode, 1900*, 93.

6. *De Wachter*, 11 March 1896, 4. Herman Bavinck was also a son of the churches of the Secession of 1834 in The Netherlands. He first taught dogmatics in the Theological School at Kampen and then accepted an appointment to teach the same subject in 1902 at the Free University of Amsterdam.

7. *Acta der Synode, 1902*, 26; *De Wachter*, 25 July 1902, 1.

8. *De Wachter*, 11 June 1957, 5.

9. Ibid.

10. Cf. G. D. De Jong, "The History of the Development of the Theological School," in *Semi-Centennial Volume* (Grand Rapids: Published for the Semi-Centennial Committee of the Theological School and Calvin College, 1926), 37.

11. *Acta der Synode, 1906*, 34.

12. *The Banner*, 14 September 1906, 233.

13. Louis Berkhof, *Beknopte Bijbelsche Hermeneutiek* (Kampen: J. H. Kok, 1911), 1-209.

14. *De Wachter*, 10 December 1913, 5.

15. Louis Berkhof, *The Church and Social Problems* (Grand Rapids: Eerdmans-Sevensma, 1913), 3, 4, 9-12, 16-20.

16. Ibid., 16-20.

17. *Acta der Synode, 1914*, 27. After not being reappointed in 1906, Janssen studied in Germany, Scotland, and The Netherlands. He also completed a course of studies qualifying him for candidacy for the ministry at the Free University of Amsterdam. According to G. D. De Jong, the synod presumed that Dr. Janssen had "learned a great deal since 1906" (De Jong, "History," 41).

18. The synod did not completely agree with Berkhof. It advised Christian laborers, if they were compelled to join neutral unions in order to provide for themselves, powerfully to witness by word and deed within the unions to the fact that they belonged to Christ and sought his honor. *Acta der Synode, 1916*, 38-39. This was the only major issue in the Christian Reformed Church during Berkhof's life on which Berkhof and the synod differed.

19. Henry Bultema, *Maranatha: Eene Studie Over de Onvervulde Profetie* (Maranatha: A Study Concerning Unfulfilled Prophecy) (Grand Rapids: Eerdmans-Sevensma, 1917).

20. The reason is obvious. The synod was to meet in June and many synodical delegates could read and understand Dutch better than English.

21. Louis Berkhof, *Premillennialisme* (Grand Rapids: Eerdmans-Sevensma, 1918), 18-29.

22. Ibid., 30-40.

23. Ibid., 41-46.

24. Ibid., 52-53.

25. For a more complete history of the controversy, see John H. Krom-

minga, *The Christian Reformed Church: A Study in Orthodoxy* (Grand Rapids: Baker Book House, 1949), 72-74.

26. The letter is reproduced in F. M. Ten Hoor, W. Heyns, L. Berkhof, and S. Volbeda, *Nadere Toelichting omtrent De Zaak Janssen* (A Closer Look Concerning the Janssen Case) (Holland: Holland Printing Company, n.d.), 3.

27. Ibid., 34-63.

28. Ibid., 63-80.

29. Ibid., 82-83.

30. R. Janssen, *Voortzetting Van Den Strijd* (Continuing the Struggle) (Grand Rapids: n.p., 1922), 4-6.

31. Letter of Janssen to the synod, *Acta der Synode, 1922*, 27.

32. *Acta der Synode, 1922*, 270-78. For a more detailed history of the Janssen Case see Kromminga, *Christian Reformed Church*, 75-79.

33. The two most prominent were Quirinus Breen and R. B. Kuiper. Breen later was awarded a Ph.D. degree in church history from the University of Chicago and taught for many years at the University of Oregon. R. B. Kuiper, Janssen's brother-in-law, went to the Reformed Church in America. Without acknowledging he had made a mistake, Kuiper recanted positively and profusely in *As to Being Reformed* (Grand Rapids: Wm. B. Eerdmans Publishing Company, 1926). Kuiper later was appointed president of Calvin College (1930), professor of practical theology at Westminster Seminary (1933), and president of Calvin Seminary (1953).

34. *Minutes of the Board of Trustees*, June 1919.

35. *Acta der Synode, 1922*, 47.

36. *Acta der Synode, 1924*, 145-47. For a brief history of the controversy see Kromminga, *Christian Reformed Church*, 82-86.

37. *Acta der Synode, 1924*, 32.

38. Clarence Bouma, "Retirement," *Calvin Forum*, October 1944, 35.

39. *The Banner*, 23 October 1925, 676.

40. Louis Berkhof, *Introductory Volume to Systematic Theology*, rev. ed. (Grand Rapids: Wm. B. Eerdmans Publishing Company, 1941), 38, 60.

41. *Acta der Synode, 1926*, 107.

42. Ten Hoor was a vigorous proponent of the infralapsarian position and stridently opposed to Kuyper. Berkhof correctly represented the supra- and infralapsarian positions on the question of the logical order of the decrees. He did not consider the two views as absolutely antithetical and rendered the opinion that both were necessarily inconsistent yet compatible with Reformed confessional orthodoxy. He did not, however, indicate that historically the two positions came to represent very different systems of theology touching many doctrinal points. Cf. *Systematic Theology* (Grand Rapids: Wm. B. Eerdmans Publishing Company, 1941), 118-25.

43. Report of the Board of Trustees, *Acts of Synod, 1932*, 207-08.

44. *The Banner*, 11 September 1931, 791-92, 806.

45. Berkhof does not comment on Reinhold Niebuhr in his books on systematic theology. For his evaluation of Niebuhr's theology see his reviews of *The Nature and Destiny of Man*, in *The Banner*, 24 September 1943, 792, and of *Christianity and Power Politics*, in *The Banner*, 23 May 1941, 504.

46. Berkhof, *Introductory Volume*, 35-36, 61, 136, and his *History of Christian Doctrines* (Grand Rapids: Wm. B. Eerdmans Publishing Company, 1937), 25.

47. Berkhof, *Introductory Volume*, 58, 60.

48. Berkhof quite simply considered any systematized body of knowledge a science (ibid., 47).

49. Ibid., 61-62, 67-68, 72, 97, 181.

50. Ibid., 23, 37, 64.

51. Ibid., 89.

52. Ibid., 17. Berkhof's major theological works were published in condensed form for college students with the title *Manual of Reformed Doctrine* (1933). In 1938 the *Manual* was further reduced for use by high-school students. It carried the title *Summary of Christian Doctrine*.

53. Berkhof, *Introductory Volume*, 58-59.

54. For examples of the extent of Berkhof's dependence on Bavinck compare Bavinck's discussion of the nature of special revelation in *Gereformeerde Dogmatiek* (Kampen: J. H. Kok, 1918), 1:362, with Berkhof's treatment of the same subject in his *Introductory Volume*, 139-40, and Bavinck's view on the wisdom of God in 2:195-96 with Berkhof's view (*Systematic Theology*, 68-69).

55. Much of the material from Berkhof's unpublished Stone Lectures was presented in this work. Berkhof was still appreciative of the social conception of the Kingdom of God articulated in the Social Gospel for correcting the older one-sided individualism and one-sided eschatological understanding of the Kingdom. Now, however, he found serious fault with the modern theological underpinnings of the Social Gospel (Louis Berkhof, *The Kingdom of God* [Grand Rapids: Wm. B. Eerdmans Publishing Company, 1951], 73-85).

56. *The Banner*, 22 April 1949, 501.

57. H. Henry Meeter listed the following: Fuller Theological Seminary, Columbia Theological Seminary, Louisville Presbyterian Seminary, Southern Baptist Theological Seminary, Gordon Divinity School, Gordon College of Theology and Missions, Western Theological Seminary, Erskine College and Theological Seminary, Northeastern Bible Institute, Providence-Barrington Bible College, Bob Jones University, and Moody Bible Institute (*De Wachter*, 11 June 1957, 14).

3

HERMAN DOOYEWEERD IN NORTH AMERICA

C. T. McINTIRE

Herman Dooyeweerd

Dooyeweerd and the Institute for Christian Studies

When surveying the Reformed tradition in Christian thought, we quite naturally turn to theologians and theology. And, indeed, all the other thinkers treated in this volume are known for their theology. But, as in the Roman Catholic tradition, there is in Reformed thought a strong and vital tradition of Christian philosophy. It is here that we meet Herman Dooyeweerd (1894-1977) in North America.[1]

In this essay I shall first examine Dooyeweerd's thought as introduced in North America, and then see what happened to his thought in the next generation in North America, especially in a group of philosophers and philosophically minded scholars influenced by Dooyeweerd and associated in one way or another with what is now known as the Institute for Christian Studies in Toronto. Unlike some of the other essays in this volume, our survey will take us right up to the present day.

Dooyeweerd was a legal scholar and philosopher at the Free University of Amsterdam from 1926 until his retirement in 1965. His most significant work was A New Critique of Theoretical Thought (4 vols.), published in its definitive form in English in North America between 1953 and 1958.[2]

Immediately after the publication of this work he traveled twice to North America, once in the fall of 1958 and again in the spring of 1959. The 1959 visit included a lecture tour of several universities and colleges, beginning with Harvard, as well as some public lectures for general audiences. The result was the book based on his lectures, In the Twilight of Western Thought (1960), written in English. Twilight is probably Dooyeweerd's best introduction to his own thought.[3] The 1958 visit included a meeting with the board of the Institute's ancestor organization, then only recently established in Ontario, known as the Association for Reformed Scientific Studies (ARSS). The result there was Dooyeweerd's suggestion to the ARSS that they write a new creed, an educational creed, that would affirm Christian principles directly germane to scholarship and higher education.[4]

Dooyeweerd's thought had been known in North America before the mid-1950s. Notably, he had published a brief earlier work in English, *Transcendental Problems of Philosophic Thought* (1948),[5] and Cornelius Van Til of Westminster Theological Seminary had spoken of Dooyeweerd's work to his students in the 1930s. Eventually two North American philosophers, David Freeman and William S. Young, working with Dooyeweerd and an English teacher from The Netherlands, collaborated to produce the new English version we know as the *New Critique*.[6] This, together with his two visits, established Dooyeweerd's presence in North America from the 1950s onward.

His thought became a noticeable element in circles associated with the Christian Reformed Church (CRC). At Calvin College, the CRC's official college, Professor H. Evan Runner became the able advocate of Dooyeweerd's thought.[7] Runner had gone to Holland at Van Til's suggestion and studied with Dooyeweerd and his colleague (and brother-in-law), the philosopher D. H. T. Vollenhoven.[8] Runner's channels at Calvin were his lectures to large classes in the Philosophy Department and his charismatic leadership of a student club, the Groen van Prinsterer Society. Runner founded the club in 1953 and attracted mainly students whose families had recently immigrated to Canada from The Netherlands. Dooyeweerd's thought also had strong supporters in two new independent colleges in the CRC orbit, Dordt College in Iowa, established in 1955, and Trinity Christian College in Illinois, founded in 1959.[9] Periodicals associated with the CRC took notice of Dooyeweerd, including the *Calvin Forum* and the *Torch and Trumpet*. The Reformed Fellowship, a CRC laymen's group that published *Torch and Trumpet*, sponsored Dooyeweerd's 1959 lecture tour.

The chief focus of interest in Dooyeweerd's thought, however, was the new Association for Reformed Scientific Studies (ARSS). It had been founded in 1956 by a small group of Dutch immigrants, both lay and clergy, in the CRC for the purpose of establishing in Canada an institution of higher learning on the model of the Free University of Amsterdam. The educational creed that Dooyeweerd had suggested in 1958 appeared in 1961. It was written by Vollenhoven, Dooyeweerd's brother-in-law, together with Professor Runner. The ARSS sponsored student conferences starting in 1959 and published the lectures first in a series known as *Christian Perspectives*, and in later years in books. In 1967 the ARSS changed its name to the Association for the Advancement of Christian Scholarship (AACS) and founded the Institute for Christian Studies in Toronto (ICS). The Institute, modeled on the interdisciplinary Philosophical Institute of the Free University, offered seminars, gradually constructed a curriculum, gathered a small faculty of eight or nine members, named another seven nonresident fellows, and eventually awarded master's degrees in philosophy. In 1983 ICS received Royal Assent to a Charter from the Parliament of Ontario, and the AACS formally ceased to exist, leaving the ICS to carry on.[10]

Since 1956 scholars associated with the ICS and its antecedents have written a sizable body of books and articles for both scholarly and nonscholarly audiences. No one thinker has emerged as predominant. Instead, their writings might be called the workings of a community of scholars. These works comprise much of the scholarship of the next generation after Dooyeweerd in North America.[11]

This next generation has passed through three phases.[12] The first phase, during the 1950s and 1960s, consisted chiefly of translating Dutch scholarship into English, bringing Dutch scholars to North America, sending North American students to Amsterdam, and promoting Dooyeweerd's thought with the enthusiasm and aggressiveness that disciples have for their master. The second phase, from the late 1960s to the late 1970s, included converting the Institute into a serious academic community, taking the first important steps of independence from Dooyeweerd's thought yet continuing in the tradition of Dooyeweerd, and opening up differences between conservative and progressive emphases among the broad group of scholars who related to Dooyeweerd's thought. The third phase, since the late 1970s, has featured the production of new scholarship that in general continued the tradition of Christian thought identified with Dooyeweerd, while being fully involved in contemporary scholarship within the academic world at large. Often significant differences continued to appear among those who related to Dooyeweerd's tradition. Through this process of transmutation the scholars in this broad group sought to sift the enduring from the ephemeral.

Dooyeweerd's Thought

Dooyeweerd presented the primary elements of his thought in *A New Critique of Theoretical Thought*.[13] That work itself was a revised edition based on a translation of his three-volume *De Wijsbegeerte der Wetsidee (The Philosophy of the Law-Idea)* published in Holland in 1935-36. Altogether Dooyeweerd published more than 200 books and articles in the fields of law, political theory, and philosophy. His thought touched a wide range of areas—ontology, epistemology, social philosophy, philosophy of history, aesthetics, philosophy of science, legal theory, political philosophy, the history of law, theology, and the history of philosophy. He was a comprehensive thinker with an amazing versatility, and his ideas were capable of inspiring thought in almost any field of learning. As a system builder he may be compared with philosophers Jacques Maritain and Bernard Lonergan, theologian Paul Tillich, historian Arnold Toynbee, and social theorists Talcott Parsons and Pitrikim Sorokin. He sought to continue the Christian tradition of the great Dutch thinker and prime minister of the preceding generation, Abraham Kuyper (1901-1905).

Dooyeweerd claimed that he wrote, not theology, but philosophy informed by Christian insights. As such, he wrote not about God but about the general structure of the world and human existence. The characteristic elements of his thought may be grouped under the following themes: 1. religion; 2. creation, fall, and redemption; 3. modal theory; 4. individuality theory; and 5. the opening process of history.

1. Religion. [14] Dooyeweerd understood religion to be the supreme motive of human existence. He contended that we are related either to God in the totality of our being or to an idol, an alternative to God whether transcendent or this-worldly. Accordingly, religion is not a distinct department of life or something that we can do without if we so choose. Understood in this way, every human being is religious, and nothing that we do in life is separable from religion. All of life is from God, dependent upon God, and responsive to God.

According to Dooyeweerd, religion is integrative and central to life. Our religion is rooted in our hearts as the manifestation of our unity, what the Scriptures call our soul or spirit. He rejected all notions of a dualism between soul and body, and instead interpreted soul as the unifying totality of our being as related to God or a substitute.

Religion is the basic dynamic, the "ground motive," of our lives. God calls us and we respond, but not always in ways faithful to the will of God. Dooyeweerd, following St. Augustine, believed that there are two great types of this "ground motive"—the Spirit of God and the Spirit of the Evil One. He suggested that these have been translated into four specific ground motives—the Greek-Roman pagan motive of form and matter; the Christian motive of creation, fall, and redemption; the originally medieval motive of grace and nature that seeks a synthesis between pagan and Christian religion; and the secular humanist motive of freedom and nature. Thinkers empowered according to this modern secular motive, such as Immanuel Kant, are certain that "religion" is not relevant to theoretical thought and that reason is autonomous. The basic thesis of Dooyeweerd's "new critique" of theoretical thought is that belief in the autonomy of reason is a pretension that cannot hide the religious character of all thought.

2. Creation, Fall, and Redemption. This is the religious ground motive that is consonant with the Scriptures. Dooyeweerd explained its meaning in this way: *creation* denotes that all of reality is God's, a disclosure of his will, and good; *fall* indicates our radical resistance to the love of God and love of our neighbor, because of which our existence as God's creatures is filled with suffering and evil; *redemption* turns us to Jesus Christ by whom we may be radically restored to God and our neighbors, and the whole creation may become as it ought to be, the recreation of God.

Dooyeweerd regarded his entire philosophy as an attempt to manifest the dynamic of this Christian religious motive in theoretical terms. He conceived of theory as an explication of the law-structure of creation. He emphasized the conflict among the fruits of the two Spirits—of God and of the Evil One—as the "antithesis" due to the Fall that divided thought from thought and persons from persons, even as it cut through the lives of Christians. He stressed that the structures of creation were norms by which God called us to do what is healthy and to work out by means of human action the redemption that Jesus Christ accomplished.

3. *Modal Theory.*[15] The first of two ways in which Dooyeweerd conceptualized reality was in his modal theory. In this he explicitly sought to expand upon the idea of "sphere sovereignty" put forward by Kuyper. Whereas in religion we tend toward the integration and unity of our lives, in the actual expression of our lives we manifest diversity. As Dooyeweerd depicted it, reality is temporal, and cosmic time, like a prism, refracts the unity of the one light into many diverse modes of existence. The modes are aspects of reality, the many different ways in which an entity exists or an act occurs. The modal aspects are, on one side, structures or laws of creation; on the other, they are the various ways in which we exist historically, no one of which is reducible to any other.

Dooyeweerd provisionally identified fifteen modal aspects of reality, including the numerical, biotic, psychical, lingual, jural, and pistic (faith). Each aspect revealed a law or norm that characterized the aspect. For example, the biotic law is organic growth, the lingual norm is symbolic signification, and the jural norm is justice. Dooyeweerd worked out a very elaborate system by which he explained how each aspect referred by analogy to every other aspect, networking the aspects of reality in a complex but magnificent integration. He showed how each scholarly discipline pertained especially to a unique aspect, such as biology to the biotic, linguistics to the lingual, and theology to the pistic. Philosophy had the task of overall integration, such as by theorizing about the modes and their interrelations as a whole, while each science treated its own aspect within the context of philosophical interrelations.

4. *Individuality Theory.*[16] While his modal theory looked at *aspects* of reality—e.g., biotic, jural, pistic—his individuality theory analyzed

whole phenomena of reality—e.g., trees, states, and churches. Whereas by means of modality analysis he identified specific kinds of aspects of entities, by means of individuality analysis he identified kinds of entities.

The important issue is to apprehend the unique and irreducible character of each modal aspect or each kind of entity. For example, in modal theory faith (pistic) manifests a unique character according to the norm of faith (transcendental certainty) and may not be reduced to the social or psychic aspects of faith. In individuality theory churches are communities properly characterized by faith and may not rightly be treated as merely social or economic in character, although those aspects are also present. Dooyeweerd was thus both a pluralist and an antireductionist; he accepted the diversity of created reality as basic.

His individuality theory enabled him to explain how there could be different kinds of entities, yet how each kind could exhibit every aspect of reality. For example, states such as France and Canada are characteristically jural communities united around the jural norm of justice. At the same time, states exhibit spatial, economic, social, and all the other modal aspects. They do so in ways that belong to a jurally qualified institution. Thus, states do not exist to make a profit or to create friendships, but to maintain justice. In this light, Dooyeweerd regards it as proper for states in the name of justice to redistribute wealth among the citizenry from the richer to the poorer members. Likewise, an industry such as General Motors Corporation rightly exists when it acts according to the characteristic norm of stewardly saving care for the human and natural resources of creation. While GM needs to match income with expenditure, even here the aim should not be to make profit, but act according to that norm of stewardship, in relation to all the other aspects of reality, including the aesthetic quality of the workplace and the equity of the decision-making process.

According to his theory, people express their religion directly by means of their response to the norm appropriate to each different kind of entity.

5. *History.* [17] Dooyeweerd's philosophy of history provided the invisible backbone of his whole system of thought. The elements of his philosophy of history were scattered, however. He regarded his theory of time as the basis of his system. It was an unusual notion of time. He called it cosmic time, and identified it as the pluriform diversity of the modal aspects. He contrasted it with the unity and coherence of reality as centered in the human heart, which he treated as supratemporal (beyond time). As a result there were different sorts of time, for example, linguistic time, astronomic time, or jural time.

What he called the historical aspect was merely one appearance of time as past, present, and future. The historical aspect he supposed was one mode among the fifteen he identified. It had to do with power, control, or mastery, and he sometimes called it the cultural mode. He believed that historical study specialized in analysis of the historical mode of any thing.

This historical mode served as the foundation or starting point for a very complicated process, called "the opening process," that swept through the modes in the actual course of any thing's history. By means of the opening process, static or closed cultures were made to develop by means of differentiation, individualization, and new integration. In this manner Dooyeweerd believed the world could unfold in fulfillment of the cultural mandate of Genesis 1. History would become a process of development initiated by faith. Dooyeweerd's vision of history was sweeping, and he linked it directly to St. Augustine's vision of the two cities in struggle for the course of history.

Many other elements of Dooyeweerd's thought, particularly in epistemology and philosophical anthropology, could be mentioned, but these five are both central and characteristic enough to indicate the thrust of his work.

The Generation after Dooyeweerd

When Dooyeweerd's work appeared in North America in the 1950s, a number of scholars took notice of it in books and articles. William S. Young, one of the translators of the *New Critique*, was the first, and he referred to it in his book *Towards a Reformed Philosophy* (1952). The second translator, David H. Freeman, completed a doctoral dissertation at the University of Pennsylvania, partly on Dooyeweerd (1958), and he published *Recent Studies in Philosophy and Theology* (1962) in which he compared Dooyeweerd with Étienne Gilson, Jacques Maritain, and Paul Tillich. Ronald Nash wrote *Dooyeweerd and the Amsterdam Philosophy* (1962), and Arthur Holmes included Dooyeweerd in *Christian Philosophy in the Twentieth Century* (1969). Rousas John Rushdoony discussed Dooyeweerd in several essays, including his Introduction to Dooyeweerd's *In The Twilight of Western Thought* (1960).[18]

These and many other writings contributed to an awareness of Dooyeweerd's thought. Evan Runner and the Association for Reformed Scientific Studies (ARSS) in Ontario, however, sought to go the next step and act on Dooyeweerd's thought. Runner and his Groen van Prinsterer Society at Calvin College inspired Hendrik Hart, Bernard Zylstra, James Olthuis, and Arnold De Graaff to go to the Free University of Amsterdam for their doctoral studies. Dooyeweerd supervised Zylstra's dissertation on Harold Laski's political theory. Hart went into general philosophy, writing on John Dewey's epistemology. Olthuis wrote on ethics and theology, and De Graaff wrote on psychology and education. Calvin Seerveld, only indirectly influenced by Runner at Calvin, went to Amsterdam earlier on his own to work under Vollenhoven, completing a dissertation on Benedetto Croce's aesthetics.[19] These five became the first members of the faculty of the Institute for Christian Studies after it opened in 1967.

The other avenue of Runner's influence was the series of annual student conferences begun by the ARSS in 1959 in Ontario. Runner's lectures at the first two were published separately by the ARSS in 1960 and 1961 and eventually put together as a book, *The Relation of the Bible to Learning* (1967).[20] Runner's themes were all Dooyeweerd's—religion, the ground-motives and the religious antithesis, sphere sovereignty and the modal theory, and the law of God in creation.

But some recognizably new emphases appeared in Runner's version of some of these themes. Chief of these was his stress on the Word of God, by which he meant the Bible. Dooyeweerd's emphasis, it may be said, was always on Creation-Order as a reality in the context of which the Scriptures were needed as a guide. Runner reversed the emphasis, in keeping with his North American Evangelical and Reformed experience, and made the Bible the centerpiece. Parallel with this, Runner stressed the religious character of everything under the new banner of "life is religion," and, in contrast with Dooyeweerd, put less emphasis on the theoretical analysis of reality. Thirdly, Runner accented the "religious antithesis," the utter opposition in thought and scholarship between the way of God and all other spirits. Dooyeweerd, by contrast, while working with the notion of religious antithesis in the sense of St. Augustine, had stressed creating his own system of thought in debate with other kinds of thought. Fourthly, Runner transformed the notion of working with Dooyeweerd's thought into a mission that Dutch Calvinistic youth in North America should especially undertake. With this he reversed the trend in Dooyeweerd from his accentuated Calvinism in the 1920s and 1930s to his ecumenical Christian thought based on the common scriptural message in the 1950s. (Dooyeweerd desired to change the name of his thought from Calvinistic philosophy to the more general term Christian philosophy.) By means of these four new emphases, Runner helped to create a small movement possessing an élan and a compelling purpose.

The founding of the Institute for Christian Studies in Toronto implemented Dooyeweerd's thought in a most tangible way. His thought was not made official, so to speak, but it did serve as the unwritten basis for interdisciplinary scholarly discourse within the Institute. It offered a model with two applications—first, for the intrinsic integration of Christian insight with scholarly thought, and second, for the identification and interrelation of all fields of scholarly study. The character and curriculum of the Institute reflected both applications at once.[21] The Institute regarded itself from the start as a *philosophical* rather than a theological school. Following Dooyeweerd, it regarded each field of academic study as resting upon a philosophical basis in which fundamental decisions were made about human nature, the purpose of life, and the character of reality. And such matters are the very ones that Christian insights directly illuminated. The Institute adopted Dooyeweerd's theory that philosophy by definition was an integrative endeavor, with respect to which Christian insights concerning the wholeness and integrity of reality were directly relevant.

By the early 1970s the Institute created two core courses—biblical foundations and philosophical foundations. In so doing it stressed that the Scriptures were not the special document of theology students and biblical scholars, but the integrative and directive religious source for the insights basic to any field of study. Thus philosophy, pursued according to biblical insights, served to ground and orient each academic field. For the rest, they added courses in the philosophy of as many fields as they could, given the limits of financial resources and personnel.

In the late 1970s the Institute faculty numbered nine scholars who taught in the areas of philosophy, history of philosophy, theology, philosophical theology, philosophy of history, political theory, economic and social philosophy, psychological theory, and philosophical aesthetics. The course of study was rounded out by a second-year interdisciplinary seminar that involved most fields, and by research on master's theses.

The Institute was founded with two clear mandates: to pursue the religious reformation of various scholarly fields, and to pursue academic research.[22] Both aims—reformation and research—were by definition inclined toward innovation. But both also required a stable institutional format and a stable relation with the supporting constituency. These needs for innovation and stabilization could—and did—often conflict. I have already referred to three phases in the Institute's history—the aggressive, the settling down, and the academically productive phases. These can now be paraphrased as the transition from being a movement to being a scholarly institution. Both founding mandates, actively pursued, were conducive to such a transition.

Included in the transition was a new relation to Dooyeweerd's thought. Whereas at the beginning the Institute depended on Dooyeweerd, by the late 1970s the faculty members had each moved to fresh terrain but always with Dooyeweerd's thought in the background. It is possible to review the five thematic elements of Dooyeweerd's thought surveyed earlier and observe what became of them in the teaching and writings of the Institute's faculty. The most important work for this comparison is a volume of essays entitled *The Legacy of Herman Dooyeweerd: Reflection on Critical Philosophy in the Christian Tradition* (1985).[23] The essays were written by six authors who were faculty members of the Institute. Of the many other writings by Institute scholars, especially notable are Hendrik Hart's *Understanding Our World: An Integral Ontology* (1984) and Calvin Seerveld's *Rainbows for the Fallen World: Aesthetic Life and Artistic Task* (1980).[24]

Two general observations may be made at the outset.[25] First, Dooyeweerd's system as a whole has not been taken over by the next generation. This may mean no more than observing that only Dooyeweerd could maintain Dooyeweerd's system, and that any subsequent thinkers who tried to do so would become scholastic disciples and not a group of scholars with their own contributions to make. Second, what did continue were some general orientations and some general themes and insights of a philosophically relevant kind concerning what was important and how to proceed in philosophy. These observations will become concrete as we review the five themes.

1. Religion. Institute members would agree that Dooyeweerd made his point about the religious basis of theoretical thought, indeed of all human activity. All humans are religious and as such their lives are oriented toward God or some substitute. Thus, the relation between religion and scholarship is intrinsic and integral.

They would grant, further, that religion is a motivating power, but it appears that no Institute scholar continues to work with the idea of religious ground-motives in Western civilization. None would carry on Dooyeweerd's extensive analysis of the polar tensions within the ground motives by which he interpreted the history of culture and philosophy. None would regard the heart as distinguishable from the whole of our person and our functioning; some have suggested that Dooyeweerd created a new dualistic view of our human make-up, in spite of his best intentions.

2. Creation, Fall, and Redemption. All the Institute scholars would regard this as an insightful summary of the central theme of the Scriptures concerning the world. But they would differ about whether it should be treated as a "ground motive" as did Dooyeweerd in the 1950s, or merely as a theme, or triad of themes, as Dooyeweerd did in the 1920s and 1930s. They all would regard an understanding of reality as creation, structured and good, as basic to Christian philosophizing. Likewise, they would understand the work of Jesus Christ as re-creation and in principle culturally pervasive in overcoming the effects of evil and suffering.

3. Modal Theory. All would agree that some sort of modal analysis is useful and valid to account for the constitutional diversity of reality.

Indeed, modal analysis would be taken as the chief means of identifying and interrelating the various distinct academic disciplines. But Institute scholars differ on what the modes may be, what their characterizing norms may be, and to what degree modal analysis is useful.

Some regard modal theory as useful first of all merely as an indicator of ontologically irreducible diversity. Others actively pursue modal analysis. For example, Olthuis stays fairly close to Dooyeweerd's version of the aspect of faith as transcendental certainty, calling it simply certitude. He agrees that theology is a special theoretical discipline focused on the mode of faith (certitude). Seerveld thinks Dooyeweerd is right about an aesthetic mode and aesthetics as a special science, but he rejects Dooyeweerd's understanding of aesthetics as having to do with harmony and beauty. He works instead with notions of allusiveness and imagination. Probably all would reject Dooyeweerd's proposal that there is a historical mode, and would work instead toward a more embracive understanding of history. Hart makes the move of conceiving of the modes, not as aspects, an idea that has static and spatial connotations, but as functions, calling up active and operational suggestions. All would agree that philosophy is best treated as an integrative as well as an analytic discipline, charged with conceptualizing the bases and interrelations of all the scholarly fields.

4. *Individuality Theory.* Probably all would think that theorizing about the structure of individual entities is important. Hart calls such phenomena "functors" and discusses functions (modal) as what functors do. But he does not pursue the theme of functors as fully as he does modal functions. Seerveld distinguishes art works as individual entities that are aesthetic in character from the aesthetic aspect of other nonaesthetic entities (such as someone's home).

On the whole, scholarly attention to individuality theory is slight compared with attention to modal theory. All would, however, stress the importance of a pluralist social theory that honored the distinctive yet interrelated character of each kind of social institution and relationship—churches, governments, colleges, neighborhoods, cities, labor unions, families, and so on.

5. *History.* I have already mentioned that all would reject the notion that history could be accounted for by means of Dooyeweerd's historical mode. All would also reject Dooyeweerd's theory of the heart as supratemporal, above and beyond time and history. They would disagree about whether time should be regarded as synonymous with ordered diversity (as in Dooyeweerd), or more pervasively identified as process and past-present-future relations. And they would disagree about the value of Dooyeweerd's theory of the opening process. The judgment

from the historian's angle has been that Dooyeweerd's theory wrongly elevates development above all other processes of history. What is needed is more theorizing about the great variety of temporal-historical processes, and this in a wide multi-cultural way. Dooyeweerd's relating of history to the cultural mandate of Genesis 1 would seem insightful as a way of identifying human responsibilities in history making, but more subtlety and actual historical analysis would be needed in order to create a more flexible philosophy of history influenced by Christian insights.

Conclusion

No doubt Herman Dooyeweerd has been the most creative philosopher in the Reformed tradition thus far in the twentieth century. However, the barriers to recognizing his creativity and transposing his philosophy to North America have not been small. His categories, special language, and method were shaped in a Dutch and European religious and philosophical milieu very different from that of his North American counterparts. The prevailing North American traditions of Reformed theology and analytic philosophy were unsympathetic to his thought. The Dutch Canadian community, which has been the chief transmitter of Dooyeweerd's thought, was separated from the mainstream of academic discourse like any immigrant group. The early aspirations to build a movement with a unique and exclusive salvific message needlessly impeded normal discourse about Dooyeweerd's thought.

Nonetheless, the presence of Dooyeweerd's thought in North America has been very beneficial. Once the effort is made to become acquainted with Dooyeweerd's work, the character of his creativity is evident.

The generation after Dooyeweerd has successfully made the transition to viable, innovative scholarship in full discourse with the North American academic community as a whole. Institute scholars have meaningfully relativized Dooyeweerd while, seeking to distill the more enduring legacy he has to offer.

What may continue and be of value to others is not Dooyeweerd's system or his specific formulations, but a type of approach to scholarship. That approach may perhaps be summarized in this way: the impulse to explore reality empirically and theoretically, so that the irreducible diversity yet the coherent integration of reality is respected, that the insights of the Christian religion are intrinsic to scholarship in full discourse with the academic world, and that the results are of service to God and to all people.

Notes: Herman Dooyeweerd in North America

1. See "Christian Philosophy," *Encyclopedia Britannica* (15th edition, 1974), IV: 555-62; and *Philosophy in the 20th Century: Catholic and Christian*, ed. George F. McLean, 2 vols. (New York: Frederick Unger, 1967). We should note from the outset that there is another strong tradition of Reformed philosophy in North America that emphasizes philosophy of religion and rational discourse about claims concerning God, and that has associated with the tradition of Anglo-American thought known as analytic philosophy. In spite of differences, there are nonetheless strong affinities between philosophers in that Reformed line of thought and Dooyeweerd, chiefly by way of Dooyeweerd's predecessor Abraham Kuyper. See Hendrik Hart and Johan van der Hoeven, eds., *Rationality in the Calvinian Tradition* (Washington: University Press of America, 1983); and Alvin Plantinga and Nicholas Wolterstorff, eds., *Faith and Rationality: Reason and Belief in God* (Notre Dame: University of Notre Dame Press, 1983).

2. Dooyeweerd, *A New Critique of Theoretical Thought*, 4 vols. (Amsterdam: Paris; Philadelphia: Presbyterian and Reformed Publishing Company, 1953-1958). Hereafter *New Critique*.

3. Dooyeweerd, *In the Twilight of Western Thought* (Philadelphia: Presbyterian and Reformed Publishing Company, 1960). Hereafter *Twilight*.

4. The text of the educational creed is published in the *Academic Bulletin* of the Institute for Christian Studies.

5. Dooyeweerd, *Transcendental Problems of Philosophic Thought* (Grand Rapids: Wm. B. Eerdmans Publishing Company, 1948).

6. Freeman and Young collaborated on Volume 1, while Freeman and H. DeJongste collaborated on Volumes 2 and 3. Dooyeweerd went over the entire English version himself and revised and added sections.

7. On Runner, see John Kraay and Anthony Tol, eds., *Hearing and Doing: Philosophical Essays dedicated to H. Evan Runner* (Toronto: Wedge Publishing Company, 1979); and Henry Vander Goot, ed., *Life Is Religion: Essays in Honor of H. Evan Runner* (St. Catharines: Paideia Press, 1981).

8. On Vollenhoven, see *The Idea of Christian Philosophy: Essays in Honour of D. H. T. Vollenhoven* (Toronto: Wedge Publishing Company, 1973).

9. Two more Reformed colleges in CRC circles were founded in Canada, both with Dooyeweerd's thought as a factor, Redeemer College, Hamilton, Ontario (1982), and The King's College, Edmonton, Alberta (1979).

10. The history of the ARSS, AACS, and ICS has yet to be written. A special issue of the ICS Newsletter, *Perspective*, published in 1981 on the twenty-fifth anniversary of the founding of the ARSS, gives many interesting historical vignettes.

11. A partial list to 1975 is published in L. Kalsbeek, *Contours of a Christian Philosophy: An Introduction to Herman Dooyeweerd's Thought* (Toronto: Wedge Publishing Company, 1975), 313-39.

12. What follows is based on countless documents and personal observations over the years since 1960.

13. This treatment of Dooyeweerd's thought is based chiefly on the *New Critique*, his *magnum opus*. His published works through 1977 are listed in the back of a book that is an excellent scholarly introduction to his thought, Hendrik Van Eikema Hommes, *Inleiding tot de Wijsbegeerte van Herman Dooyeweerd* (The Hague: Martinus Nijhoff, 1982). The book by Kalsbeek, mentioned above, is also good and very readable. Other books to consult are Dooyeweerd's *Twilight*, and

his *Roots of Western Culture: Pagan, Secular, and Christian Options* (Toronto: Wedge Publishing Company, 1979).

14. Dooyeweerd treats religion, and creation, fall, redemption, in *New Critique*, Vol. 1.

15. He discusses modal theory in *New Critique*, Vol. 2.

16. Individuality theory is the subject of *New Critique*, Vol. 3.

17. Most of his philosophy of history is discussed in *New Critique*, Vol. 2, but much is scattered throughout the whole work.

18. Young, *Towards a Reformed Philosophy* (Franeker: T. Wever, 1952); Freeman, *Recent Studies in Philosophy and Theology* (Philadelphia: Presbyterian and Reformed Publishing Company, 1962); Nash, *Dooyeweerd and the Amsterdam Philosophy* (Grand Rapids: Zondervan Publishing House, 1962); Holmes, *Christian Philosophy in the Twentieth Century* (Nutley, NJ: Craig, 1969); Rushdoony, "Introduction," *Twilight*, vii-xvi.

19. Hart, *Communal Certainty and Authorized Truth* (Amsterdam: Swets and Zeitlinger, 1966); Zylstra, *From Pluralism to Collectivism* (Assen: Van Gorcum, 1968; New York: Humanities Press, 1970); Olthuis, *Facts, Values, and Ethics* (Assen: Van Gorcum, 1968; New York: Humanities Press, 1969); De Graaff, *The Educational Ministry of the Church* (Nutley, NJ: Craig, 1968); Seerveld, *Benedetto Croce's Earlier Aesthetic Theories and Literary Criticism* (Kampen: J. H. Kok, 1958).

20. Runner, *The Relation of the Bible to Learning* (Toronto: ARSS, 1967).

21. The Institute's statements of purpose and its curriculum have been presented in its *Academic Bulletin*, issued every year or two since 1967.

22. These mandates are presented in the Preamble and the Educational Creed of the ARSS (now ICS), which are printed in the ICS *Academic Bulletin*.

23. *The Legacy of Herman Dooyeweerd: Reflections on Critical Philosophy in the Christian Tradition* (Washington: University Press of America, 1985).

24. Hart, *Understanding Our World* (Washington: University Press of America, 1984); Seerveld, *Rainbows for the Fallen World* (Toronto: Tuppence Press, 1980). A full listing of publications by members of the Institute's faculty and associates may be obtained from the Institute, 229 College Street, Toronto, Ontario, M5T 1R4.

25. What follows is based on my reading of most of the publications by Institute scholars as well as firsthand knowledge of their teaching.

4

CORNELIUS VAN TIL

WESLEY A. ROBERTS

Cornelius Van Til

REFORMED theologians have been concerned not only with a correct understanding of the Christian faith but also with the rational defense and justification of Christianity's truth claims. The latter activity falls within the discipline of apologetics, long regarded as a branch of theology. Reformed theologians, however, are not agreed on the relation of apologetics to the theological encyclopedia as a whole. B. B. Warfield, for example, argued that apologetics is the discipline that establishes the knowledge of God that theology explicates.[1] Dutch theologians like Abraham Kuyper and Herman Bavinck argued that apologetics should not precede but follow upon the work of systematic theology that determines the content of the Christian faith.

Cornelius Van Til, a student of both the old Princeton school of theologians and the great Dutch Reformed thinkers, sees a mutual dependence of apologetics and systematic theology.[2] Van Til is not a systematician but an apologist with a strong commitment to Reformed theology that permeates all his writings.

Van Til is regarded by many as one of the foremost Christian apologists of our time. He is perhaps the most controversial Reformed thinker of the twentieth century, the man responsible for initiating a new approach to apologetics. At Princeton Theological Seminary, Van Til was introduced to the traditional method of apologetics espoused by giants of the theological world such as Charles Hodge, B. B. Warfield, Francis L. Patton, William Brenton Greene, Jr., and J. Gresham Machen. This method "is to present evidence and arguments from all different lines of thought in an attempt to show that God exists and that the Bible is the Word of God, and that the burden of inferential proof is so great that there is no excuse for an unbeliever to reject Christianity."[3]

During the academic year 1928-1929, while serving as instructor in apologetics at Princeton, Van Til had an opportunity to assess the apologetic methodology he had received as a student and was using as a teacher. He became convinced that this method was not consistent with the teachings of the Reformed faith. It was not, however, until he joined the faculty of the newly founded Westminster Theological Seminary in September of 1929 as Professor of Apologetics that he began to work out his new approach. Van Til's doctoral work in philosophy had made him aware of the insight of post-Kantian metaphysicians that "the given presuppositions of any philosophical position predetermined and governed much of its later outworkings."[4] When he applied this notion to the traditional apologetic method he saw that this method accepted the non-Christian presuppositions of its adversaries rather than challenged them. This led Van Til to his "pioneering insight" that in apologetics the presuppositions and not merely attendant arguments have to be biblical.[5] His reading of the writings of Abraham Kuyper and Herman Bavinck further strengthened his viewpoint that in apologetics one must not begin with human reason or some supposedly neutral position. Rather, one must begin with the presupposition that there is a God and that men are responsible to him. Information about this God is presented in the inspired Scriptures. This was the beginning of presuppositional apologetics with which Van Til's name has been identified for the past half century.

Van Til maintains an uncompromising commitment to Reformed theology. It is the Reformed expression of the Christian faith that he seeks to defend. He admits his indebtedness to the classic Reformed theologians and quotes freely from them. He is willing to go beyond them, however, in areas where he thinks they are weak. He thinks that he can best honor men such as Warfield and Kuyper by building on the main thrust of their thought rather than by carrying on what is inconsistent with their basic position.[6] Bernard Ramm has given a fine summary of Van Til's location within the Reformed faith:

> Van Til has made a sustained effort to have an apologetic system that grows naturally out of the reformed system of theology. The godfather of his system is certainly John Calvin, although he admits that Augustine was the first Christian theologian to try to work out a Christian metaphysics and epistemology. His more immediate apologetic relatives are such great Dutch thinkers as Kuyper and Bavinck and such outstanding Calvinists as Hodge and Warfield. He has had great sympathy with the Calvinistic philosophy as recently developed at the Free University of Amsterdam by Vollenhoven and Dooyeweerd.[7]

It is Van Til's conviction that in Calvinism more than any other form of Protestantism the message of Christianity is clearly presented as a challenge to the wisdom of the world.

Van Til's apologetic writings contain so much exposition of Reformed theology that critics have charged that he confuses apologetics with systematic theology.[8] This is a common misunderstanding of Van Til's position. Van Til does believe that "defense and positive statement go hand in hand" but he makes a distinction between the two.[9] The misunderstanding arises from Van Til's insistence that theology must have an apologetic thrust, and apologetics must expound theology. The difference in practice, as Frame points out, is a difference in emphasis rather than of subject matter.[10] To understand Van Til's apologetic is at the same time to understand his theology. For his epistemology is based on his metaphysics. Fundamental to his system is the Creator-creature distinction, which is kept in focus at all times. Without this basic distinction in mind one cannot grasp the significance of Van Til's position.

Christian Metaphysics

The doctrine of God is of fundamental importance to Van Til's apologetics. Everything in his system is made to turn on the existence of God. To him God is the absolute, self-conscious Being who is the source of all finite being and knowledge. Consequently, the "ontological" Trinity is made the category of interpretation for all things and the final reference point in all human thinking. The most basic fact of all facts is the existence of the triune God. Thus he asserts, "I hold that belief in God is not merely as reasonable as other belief, or even a little or infinitely more probably true than other belief; I hold rather that unless you believe in God you can logically believe in nothing else."[11]

Theologically, Van Til believes that every doctrine is bound to be false if the first and basic doctrine of God is false. "For apologetics it means that the non-Christian forms of metaphysics cannot be challenged in their basic assumptions."[12] The God of whom Van Til speaks is not one whose existence can be proved by philosophical arguments. He is the self-contained and self-sufficient God who has revealed himself in Scripture.

Unlike the old Princeton theologians who accepted the historically formulated theistic proofs, Van Til maintains that these arguments are invalid. If they were valid, he says, Christianity would not be true.[13] Van Til's point is that the non-Christian formulation of these "proofs" does not refer to the God of Scripture but to a finite god who is no God.[14] He does see value, however, in a Christian formulation of these proofs that rests on the ideas of creation and providence. As such, they appeal to what the natural man knows to be true because he is a creature of God.[15] He believes that the objective evidence for the existence of God and of the comprehensive governance of the world is so plain that men cannot get away from it. They see it about them and within them.[16]

God's existence therefore should be presented by the apologist not as "possible" or "probable," but as certain.

It is from his view of God that Van Til develops his view of reality. He believes Christianity is committed to a two-layer theory of reality or being. By this he means that God has one kind of being and the universe another kind, which is produced and sustained by God. God's being is infinite, eternal, and unchangeable; that of the universe is finite, temporal, and changeable.[17] This distinction allows him to address the philosophical problem of the one-and-many, the relation of unity to diversity. He distinguishes between the Eternal One-and-Many and the temporal one-and-many. In God unity and plurality are both ultimate and eternal. Unity is not sacrificed to plurality nor plurality to unity. The temporal one-and-many is the result of God's creation. Therefore the various aspects of created reality are made to sustain relations to one another according to the design of the Creator. He explains it as follows:

> All aspects being equally created, no one aspect of reality may be regarded as more ultimate than another. Thus the created *one and many* may in this respect be said to be *equal* to one another; they are equally derived and equally dependent upon God who sustains them both. The particulars or facts of the universe do and must act in accord with universals and laws. Thus there is order in the created universe. On the other hand, the laws may not and can never reduce the particulars to abstract particulars or reduce their individuality in any manner. The laws are but generalizations of God's method of working with particulars.[18]

Van Til seeks to be true to the Scriptures in his theory of reality. The triune God is placed at the center of his thinking and is brought to bear on every issue of philosophical importance.

Christian Epistemology

Van Til's theory of knowledge is based on his metaphysics. For there to be any validity to man's knowledge, Van Til believes we must presuppose the triune God revealed in the Bible. He believes that if the question of knowledge is made independent of the question of being, we are in effect excluding the Christian answer to the question of knowledge. Once we accept the biblical testimony with regard to God and man our knowledge will be true insofar as it corresponds with God's knowledge. The Christian, therefore, cannot be neutral to the nature of reality when he asks about the nature of knowledge.[19]

Starting with God's knowledge, Van Til argues that God's knowledge of himself and of the created universe is exhaustive. In other words, there can be no new knowledge for God about himself or the universe. God's knowledge is analytic in that he is himself the source of all that can be known. He does not add to his knowledge, which is eternal, analytic, comprehensive, and inexhaustible.[20]

From God's knowledge of himself, Van Til advances to God's knowledge of the universe. God's knowledge of the universe depends on his knowledge of himself.[21] He made the universe in accordance with his eternal plan, so its very existence depends on his knowledge. As a creature made in the image of God man can and does have true knowledge. God's knowledge is the standard of man's knowledge. "The one must be determinative and the other subordinate."[22] Van Til, however, is careful to point out that although man's knowledge of God must be true, it is not and cannot be exhaustive. Creatures cannot have comprehensive knowledge.[23]

Since man can know God truly it follows that he can also know the world truly. Van Til uses the doctrine of creation as the basis for his assertion. Since both the subject (man) and the object (created reality) of human knowledge are created by God, there must be objective knowledge. Subject and object are adapted to one another according to the plan of God. This is seen in the fact that man (subject) was given a mandate to interpret the world of objects under God. Without this interpretation of the universe by man, Van Til believes, the world would be meaningless.[24] The objectivity of knowledge, therefore, rests on the doctrine of creation. If this doctrine is relinquished, the particulars or facts of the universe would be unrelated and could not be in fruitful contact with one another.

Seeing, then, that the objects of knowledge are brought into relation with the human mind according to God's creative purpose, these objects will not be truly interpreted if they are not brought into relation with the divine mind. God being the ultimate category of interpretation, the things in the universe must be interpreted in relation to him.[25]

Van Til also points out that since God is incomprehensible to us, our knowledge, though true, is partial and always finds itself involved in paradox or seeming contradiction. "Our knowledge is analogical and therefore must be paradoxical."[26] To God there is no mystery, no paradox, but to finite man there is. God's comprehensive plan takes in all the facts but we do not need to know this plan; all we need to know is that reality is rationally controlled by God's plan.

The doctrine of revelation is important to Van Til's concept of epistemology. Since it is according to God's plan that finite things are made, Van Til insists that all knowledge that any finite creature would have must rest upon the revelation of God. Thus the knowledge that we have of the simplest objects of the physical universe is based upon the revelational activity of God.[27]

Van Til follows both Kuyper and Bavinck in stressing the fact that Scripture is *the* objective principle of knowledge for the Christian. This means that the truths of the Scriptures must be taken as the light in which all the facts of experience are to be interpreted. It follows necessarily that if Scripture holds such a crucial position its pronouncements about reality cannot be subject to the scrutiny of reason but must be taken on their own authority.[28] Van Til is aware that such a position will be criticized as authoritarian but he maintains that God's revelation is always authoritarian.[29]

> All the objections that are brought against such a position spring, in the last analysis, from the assumption that the human person is ultimate and as such should properly act as judge of all claims to authority that are made by anyone. But if man is not autonomous . . . then man should subordinate his reason to the Scriptures and seek in the light of it to interpret his experience.[30]

Van Til is opposed to both the rationalist and empiricist theories of knowledge. He criticizes Descartes for maintaining that man has knowledge within himself apart from God. Descartes's position does not recognize that all knowledge of man presupposes revelation. This also holds true for the empiricists. "Though they opposed the innate ideas of Descartes, they were no more ready to recognize the true place of revelation than was Descartes. For them the mind was a *tabula rasa*. But the mind of man as created by God cannot be a *tabula rasa*."[31] Van Til, of course, believes in innate knowledge but not in the Cartesian sense since it has no place for revelation. He sees innate knowledge as having a certain thought content, although it is involuntary and appears most clearly at the intuitional level of man's consciousness.[32] This innate knowledge does not work independently of acquired knowledge. They are correlative to one another.[33] Van Til's approach to epistemology, then, is neither inductive nor deductive, *a priori* nor *a posteriori*, as these terms have been historically understood.

Critics of Van Til have charged him with stripping men of sound intelligence. Clark Pinnock, for example, asserts that Van Til cannot escape the charge of fideism, the view that truth in religion is ultimately based on faith rather than on reasoning or evidence.[34] Pinnock, like most of his critics, misunderstands Van Til's view of the role of reason. Van Til does have a lofty concept of reason but he is careful to make reason function in total dependence on God. He believes reason is a gift given by God to man in order that he might order the revelation of God for himself. But it was never meant to function by itself without relationship to authoritative supernatural revelation.[35]

The law of contradiction is, for Van Til, the expression on a created level of the internal coherence of God's nature. He insists that the Christian should never appeal to this law as something capable of deciding what is possible or impossible. Rather,

> Christians should employ the law of contradiction, whether negatively or positively, as a means by which to systematize the facts of revelation; whether these facts are found in the universe at large or in the Scriptures. The law of contradiction cannot be thought of as operating anywhere except against the background of the nature of God.[36]

This position is set in sharp contrast to the position of the non-Christian that assumes that logic is a timeless, impersonal principle. Van Til points out that on the non-Christian assumptions no intelligible assertions can be made about the world of reality, which is really a world of chance. The non-Christian is bound to fall into self-contradictions since no assertions can be made about chance.[37]

In pointing out the dilemma of the natural man, Van Til does not intend to belittle the intellectual ability of the non-Christian. He wants merely to point out that non-Christian philosophy ought to admit that there is a dimension of reality that is beyond its reach and therefore it ought to listen to the voice of authority. Van Til admits that non-Christians often do have brilliant minds.

> We may greatly admire such a mind for what, in spite of its basic principle and because of the fact that God has released its powers in his restraining grace, it has done. For all that it must not be forgotten that this mind is still, be its name Aristotle, a covenant-breaker in Adam.[38]

However skillful the non-Christian may be in his use of logic, Van Til believes that once revelation is excluded he is bound to arrive at a conclusion contrary to the truth. He cites the example of Aristotle, who knew how to use logic. Aristotle, however, came to the conclusion that God is not the creator of man, knows nothing, and is not a person. "His conclusion was consistent with his premise. His logic was involved in his metaphysics as his metaphysics was involved in his logic."[39] It is Van Til's position therefore that revelation should not be presented for the judgment of the natural man, for every logical activity in which any man engages is in the service of his total vision.[40]

Starting Point and Methodology in Apologetics

The question of where one begins in presenting the claims of Christianity has been much debated since Van Til introduced his "new approach" to apologetics. It is Van Til's firm belief that the question of starting point is largely determined by one's theology. Thus he consistently sets the Reformed faith over against Roman Catholicism and Arminianism.

As a presuppositionalist, Van Til starts with the presupposition of the existence of God. His doctrine of God requires that it be made foundational to everything else as a principle of explanation. "If God is self-sufficient then he alone is self-explanatory. And if he alone is self-explanatory then he must be the final reference point in all human predication. He is like the sun from which all lights on earth derive their power of illumination."[41] The alternative to this, according to Van Til, would be to make man the final reference point, in which case he need not subject his mind to the revelation of God as absolutely authoritative for him. All that would be necessary is for man to refer to God as an expert who has had greater experience than he; but he need not make all thoughts captive to the obedience of Christ.[42]

Van Til maintains, therefore, that only on the presupposition of divine self-sufficiency and man's complete dependence can the difference between the Christian and the non-Christian points of view be clearly pointed out. The most basic difference between the two systems is to be found in their presuppositions. On the assumption of the non-Christian (that is, of human ultimacy), his system is one in which he himself occupies the place that God occupies in Christian theology.[43]

If, as Van Til points out, the Christian and non-Christian start from positions that are mutually exclusive, the question as to whether there is a point of contact for the presentation of the gospel to the non-Christian becomes one of tremendous importance. Stated differently, the issue has to do with whether there is a common point of agreement anywhere in the entire range of human discourse on which Christian and non-Christian can agree and argue their respective cases. If there is no common ground then there is no way of presenting the gospel to the mind and heart of man.

Van Til believes it is impossible to find a common area of knowledge between believers and nonbelievers unless there is agreement between them as to the nature of man himself. He bases this view on the fact that the human mind as the knowing subject makes its contribution to the knowledge it obtains. But since there is no agreement on the nature of man there can be no agreement on a common area of knowledge.[44] Therefore, epistemologically believers and nonbelievers are said to have nothing in common even though metaphysically they have all things in common.[45] Van Til admits that there is a sense in which all men have the facts "in common," since both saint and sinner are face to face with God and the universe of God. But because the sinner is like the man who wears colored glasses everything will be seen in a different light.[46]

Because Van Til refuses to compromise with the nonbeliever, he tells us that the only point of contact is that of head-on collision.[47] This does not mean that he has closed the door to the presentation of the gospel. The metaphysical point of contact is still open; it is to be found within the natural man. He tells us:

> With Calvin I find the point of contact for the presentation of the gospel to non-Christians in the fact that they are made in the image of God and as such have the ineradicable sense of deity within them. Their own consciousness is inherently and exclusively revelational of God to themselves. No one can help knowing God for in knowing himself he knows God. His self-consciousness is totally devoid of content, unless as Calvin puts it at the beginning of his *Institutes*, man knows himself as a creature before God. There are no atheistic men because no man can deny the revelational activity of the true God within him. . . . Every human being is by virtue of his being made in the image of God accessible to God. And as such he is accessible to one who without compromise presses upon him the claims of God.[48]

Van Til's position has not been without criticism. By stating in such an emphatic manner that the Christian and the non-Christian have nothing in common epistemologically, he has been accused of being confused on the question of common knowledge.[49] He is also accused of making unregenerate man totally devoid of knowledge.[50] These criticisms, however, are not valid, for Van Til does recognize the fact that the natural man is not always consistent with his antitheistic principle of interpretation. He constantly introduces the term "in principle" to qualify his statements about the natural man. He says very clearly that as long as the natural man *self-consciously* works from his satanic principle he can have no notion in common with the believer because the unbeliever's epistemology is informed by his ethical hostility to God.[51] Van Til, however, tells us that in the course of history the natural man is *not fully* self-conscious of his own position. Like the prodigal he cannot altogether stifle his father's voice. There is a conflict of notions within him of which he is not fully conscious. The principle of autonomy seeks to suppress his knowledge of God, and the restraining power of God's common grace seeks to suppress the principle of autonomy. This internal semiconscious conflict makes it impossible for him to proceed consistently from the one principle or the other.[52]

It is because of this situation, in which the natural man does not self-consciously work from his principles, that Van Til believes cooperation between believer and unbeliever in the field of science is possible.

Though all of the natural man's interpretations are from an ultimate point of view equally unsatisfactory, there is a sense in which he knows something about everything, about God as well as the world, and that in this sense he knows more about the world than about God. *This distinction is not only true, but important to make.* Many non-Christians have been great scientists. Often non-Christians have a better knowledge of the things of this world than Christians have.[53]

Van Til maintains this position on the ground that the world is not what non-Christians assume that it is, a world of chance, and is what Christians assume that it is, a world run by the counsel of God. It is for this reason that "even non-Christians have knowledge."[54]

Van Til's method of presenting Christianity is quite simple. Instead of trying to prove the truth of Christianity to the natural man, he assumes its truth at the outset and then challenges the presupposition of the natural man, pointing out that on his principles nothing is true, and nothing can be accounted for. Some critics view this approach as being too dogmatic. Van Til accepts this criticism because he believes God speaks to man in Scripture with absolute authority.

A Reformed method of apologetics must seek to vindicate the Reformed life and world view as Christianity come to its own. . . . This implies a refusal to grant that any area or aspect of reality, any fact or any law of nature or of history can be correctly interpreted except it be seen in the light of the main doctrines of Christianity.[55]

It is quite evident that Van Til does not present Christianity apologetically; neither does he admit that the natural man's interpretation of life is correct up to a point. Appeal to common facts is meaningless as far as he is concerned. This sets Van Til's approach at odds with the traditional method. He points out that the Romanist and Arminian views of Christianity force them to agree with the natural man in his principles of methodology to see whether or not Christian theism is true. This is due to the fact that they view the question of methodology, like that of starting point, as a neutral matter.[56] The Reformed apologist, however, cannot agree with the methodology of the natural man, which is tied up with his interpretation of himself as the ultimate reference point. Therefore, rather than utilizing the natural man's erroneous methodology in order to establish a point of contact with him for the gospel, the Reformed apologist finds his point of contact in the sense of deity that the natural man seeks to suppress. The point of contact is in the nature of a head-on collision—system with system.[57]

Van Til's method of reasoning by presupposition is controlled by his epistemological and metaphysical principles. The "ontological" Trinity is as basic to his methodology as it is to the doctrines of Christianity. Van Til's conclusion is just as fixed as his starting point. If Bertrand Russell could accuse Thomas Aquinas of possessing little of the true philosophic spirit because he knew his conclusion in advance,[58] Van Til, on this score, could be criticized for having none whatsoever. But the claim to neutrality in the investigation of truth by non-Christian thinkers is a delusion. It is this so-called neutrality, Van Til believes, that is used in an *a priori* manner to exclude the truth of Christianity before the outset of the investigation. Not to assume the truth of Christianity as a fundamental axiom in its defense would, for Van Til, be a denial of the very thing one is seeking to establish. Thus he offers no apology for his method of reasoning by presupposition.

This method of reasoning is seen by Van Til as indirect rather than direct.[59] By this he means that the issue between believers and nonbelievers relative to Christianity cannot be settled by a direct appeal to "facts" or "laws" whose nature and significance are already agreed upon by both parties in the debate. Since there is no agreement on the "facts" or "laws," the question must be settled indirectly.[60] That means the apologist is required to place himself on his opponent's position, assuming its correctness for argument's sake, in order to show him that on such a position the "facts" and the "laws" have no meaning. Conversely, the non-Christian will be asked to place himself upon the Christian position for argument's sake in order to be shown that only upon the Christian basis are "facts" and "laws" intelligible.[61] Van Til's aim is to challenge the knowledge of God that the natural man has but suppresses.

In contrast to his Reformed approach, Van Til sees the traditional method as being unable to challenge the presuppositions of the non-Christian at the outset of the argument. The reason is that "the Romanist and the evangelical are in some measure in agreement with the non-Christian on his presuppositions. They too attribute a measure of autonomy to man."[62] Van Til's conclusion is that the Romanist-evangelical method of defending Christianity has to compromise it while defending it. "As it cannot clearly show the difference between the Christian and non-Christian view of things, so it cannot present any clear-cut reason why the non-Christian should forsake his position."[63]

Even though Van Til is convinced that the non-Christian method is self-destructive, he does believe that the Reformed apologist should show interest in it. He believes the apologist should make a critical analysis of it, and even join his non-Christian friend in the use of it. "But he should do so self-consciously with the purpose of showing that its most consistent application not merely leads away from Christian theism but in leading away from Christian theism leads to destruction of reason as well as science."[64] Van Til's hope is that the non-Christian will see that Christianity is the only position that gives human reason a field for successful operation and a method of true progress in knowledge. [65]

From this one may be tempted to conclude that Van Til believes non-Christians cannot discover truth by the methods they employ, but that would be incorrect. He believes that because non-Christians are never able to employ their own methods consistently[66] they can discover truth. However, this is a discovery made

> in terms of principles that are borrowed wittingly or unwittingly from Christianity. The fact of science and its progress is inexplicable except upon the presupposition that the world is made and controlled by God through Christ and that man is made and renewed in the image of God through Christ. [67]

Throughout his career Van Til has been very critical of "the Arminian method" that has more or less characterized Protestant apologetics since the time of Bishop Joseph Butler. He believes Arminianism offers to the natural man a Christian theology with foreign elements in that it sees man as having ultimate ability to accept or reject salvation. "God has to await the election returns to see whether he is chosen as God or set aside."[68] This, Van Til believes, places the Arminian at the mercy of the natural man. For if the natural man is consistent he will tell the Arminian that "a little autonomy involves absolute autonomy, and a little reality set free from the plan of God involves all reality set free from the plan of God. After that the reduction process is simply a matter of time."[69] It should be noted here that what Van Til is criticizing is Arminianism as a system of theology and the method of apologetics employed to fit that system.

In contrast to Arminianism, Van Til believes that only in the Reformed faith can an uncompromising method of apologetics be found. "The Reformed apologist throws down the gauntlet and challenges his opponent to a duel of life and death from the start."[70] He does this because he knows that if the natural man is allowed to interpret any aspect of experience in terms of his principles without destroying the idea of intelligibility, then he has a right to claim that there is no reason why he cannot interpret the whole of experience in terms of his principles.[71] Only through reasoning by presupposition, Van Til believes, can one overcome the self-frustrating situation that the traditional method cannot avoid.

Cornelius Van Til has done a great service to apologetic methodology by seeking to develop a method that is consistent with the great doctrines of the Reformed faith. In his "epistemologically" self-conscious Calvinism he presents a consistent Christianity that effectively challenges any worldview that begins with any presupposition other than the triune God of Scripture. He boldly presents Christianity not as a worldview but as a divine system of truth that alone makes human experience intelligible and meaningful.

Notes: Cornelius Van Til

1. Benjamin B. Warfield, "Apologetics," in *The New Schaff-Herzog Encyclopedia of Religious Knowledge* (Grand Rapids: Baker Book House, 1951), 233.

2. Cornelius Van Til, *Apologetics* (Course syllabus, 1959), 3.

3. Floyd E. Hamilton, *The Basis of Christian Faith* (New York: Harper and Row, 1964), xiv.

4. William White, Jr., *Van Til: Defender of the Faith* (Nashville: Thomas Nelson, 1979), 74.

5. Ibid., 75.

6. Cornelius Van Til, *The Defense of the Faith* (Philadelphia: Presbyterian and Reformed Publishing Company, 1955), 397.

7. Bernard Ramm, *Types of Apologetic Systems* (Wheaton, IL: Van Kampen Press, 1953), 184-85.

8. In E. R. Geehan, ed., *Jerusalem and Athens* (Nutley, NJ: Presbyterian and Reformed Publishing Company, 1971), 349, 391-92.

9. Van Til, *Apologetics*, 3-4.

10. John Frame, *Van Til: The Theologian* (Phillipsburg, NJ: Pilgrim Publishing Company, 1976), 4.

11. Cornelius Van Til, *Why I Believe in God* (Philadelphia: Presbyterian and Reformed Publishing Company, n.d.), 20.

12. Van Til, *Apologetics*, 9.

13. Cornelius Van Til, *Introduction to Systematic Theology* (Course syllabus, 1961), 199.

14. Ibid., 198.

15. Van Til, *The Defense of the Faith*, 197.

16. Ibid., 254.

17. Van Til, *Apologetics*, 8.

18. Van Til, *The Defense of the Faith*, 42-44.

19. Ibid., 50.

20. Ibid., 51-52.

21. Ibid., 56.

22. Ibid.

23. Ibid., 57-58.

24. Ibid., 60.

25. Ibid., 61.

26. Ibid.

27. Ibid., 282-83.

28. Ibid., 125.

29. Ibid.

30. Ibid.

31. Van Til, *An Introduction to Systematic Theology*, 195.

32. Ibid.

33. Ibid., 197.

34. Geehan, ed., *Jerusalem and Athens*, 423.

35. Van Til, *An Introduction to Systematic Theology*, 189.

36. Ibid., 11.

37. Van Til, *The Defense of the Faith*, 143-44.

38. Ibid., 298.

39. Ibid.

40. Cornelius Van Til, *The Case for Calvinism* (Philadelphia: Presbyterian and Reformed Publishing Company, 1955), 137.

41. Cornelius Van Til, *A Christian Theory of Knowledge* (Course syllabus, 1954), 2.

42. Ibid.

43. Ibid., 4.

44. Van Til, *The Defense of the Faith*, 84.

45. Ibid., 260.

46. In B. B. Warfield, *The Inspiration and Authority of the Bible* (Philadelphia: Presbyterian and Reformed Publishing Company, 1948), 20.

47. Cornelius Van Til, *The Intellectual Challenge of the Gospel* (Phillipsburg, NJ: Lewis J. Grotennis, 1963), 19.

48. Van Til, *The Defense of the Faith*, 257.

49. Gordon H. Clark, "Apologetics," in *Contemporary Evangelical Thought*, ed. Carl F. H. Henry (New York: Channel Press, 1957), 155.

50. Ibid., 156.

51. Van Til, *The Defense of the Faith*, 189-90.

52. Ibid., 190.

53. Ibid., 286.

54. Ibid.

55. Ibid., 113.

56. Ibid., 113-14.

57. Ibid., 115-16.

58. Bertrand Russell, *A History of Western Philosophy* (New York: Simon and Schuster, 1945), 463.

59. Van Til, *Defense of the Faith*, 117.

60. Ibid.

61. Ibid., 117-18.

62. Van Til, *A Christian Theory of Knowledge*, 6.

63. Ibid.

64. Van Til, *The Defense of the Faith*, 119.

65. Ibid.

66. Ibid., 120.

67. Van Til, *The Case for Calvinism*, 106-07.

68. Van Til, *The Defense of the Faith*, 128-29.

69. Ibid., 129.

70. Ibid., 130.

71. Ibid., 198.

BIBLIOGRAPHY

1. Historical Background

Balmer, Randall H. *A Perfect Babel of Confusion: Dutch Religion and English Culture in the Middle Colonies*. New York: Oxford University Press, 1989.

Bratt, James D. *Dutch Calvinism in Modern America: A History of a Conservative Subculture*. Grand Rapids: Eerdmans, 1984.

De Jong, Gerald F. *The Dutch in America, 1609–1974*. Boston: Twayne, 1975.

De Klerk, Peter, and De Ridder, Richard, eds. *Perspectives on the Christian Reformed Church: Studies in Its History, Theology, and Ecumenicity*. Grand Rapids: Baker, 1983.

Hageman, Howard G. *Two Centuries Plus: The Story of New Brunswick Seminary*. Grand Rapids: Eerdmans, 1984.

Harmelink, Herman, III. *Ecumenism and the Reformed Church*. Grand Rapids: Eerdmans, 1968.

Kromminga, Dietrich H. *The Christian Reformed Tradition: From the Reformation to the Present*. Grand Rapids: Eerdmans, 1943.

Kromminga, John H. *The Christian Reformed Church: A Study in Orthodoxy*. Grand Rapids: Baker, 1949.

Tanis, James. *Dutch Calvinistic Pietism in the Middle Colonies*. The Hague: Martinus Nijhoff, 1968.

Van Hoeven, James W., ed. *Piety and Patriotism: Bicentennial Studies of the Reformed Church in America, 1776–1976*. Grand Rapids: Eerdmans, 1976.

Zwaanstra, Henry. *Reformed Thought and Experience in a New World: A Study of the Christian Reformed Church and Its American Environment, 1890–1918*. Kampen: J. H. Kok, 1973.

2. Netherlandic Figures

Bavinck, Herman. *Christelijke Wereldbeschouwing*. Kampen: J.H. Bos, 1904.

_____. *Gereformeerde Dogmatiek*. 4 vols. 3d ed. Kampen: Kok, 1918. (English translation of vol.2: *The Doctrine of God*. Grand Rapids: Eerdmans, 1951).

_____. *The Philosophy of Revelation*. New York: Longmans, Green, and Co., 1909.

_____. *Magnalia Dei: Onderwijzing in de Christelijke Religie naar Gereformeerde Belijdenis*. Kampen: J. H. Kok, 1909. (English translation: *Our Reasonable Faith*. Grand Rapids: Eerdmans, 1956).

Berkhof, Hendrikus. *Christ the Meaning of History*. Richmond: John Knox, 1966.

_____. *Christian Faith: An Introduction to the Study of the Faith*. Grand Rapids: Eerdmans, 1986.

Berkouwer, Gerrit C. *Studies in Dogmatics*. 18 vols. Grand Rapids: Eerdmans, 1952–1976.

_____. *The Second Vatican Council and the New Catholicism*. Grand Rapids: Eerdmans, 1965.

_____. *A Half Century of Theology*. Grand Rapids: Eerdmans, 1977.

_____. *The Triumph of Grace in the Theology of Karl Barth*. Grand Rapids: Eerdmans, 1956.

Dooyeweerd, Herman. *In the Twilight of Western Thought: Studies in the Pretended Autonomy of Philosophical Thought*. Philadelphia: Presbyterian and Reformed, 1960.

_____. *A New Critique of Theoretical Thought*. 4 vols. Amsterdam: H. J. Paris; Philadelphia: Presbyterian and Reformed, 1953–1958.

_____. *Roots of Western Culture: Pagan, Secular, and Christian Options*. Toronto: Wedge, 1979.

Kuyper, Abraham. *Encyclopedia of Sacred Theology*. New York: Charles Scribner's Sons, 1898.

_____. *De Gemeene Gratie*. 3 vols. Amsterdam: Hoveker & Wormser, 1902–1904.

_____. *Lectures on Calvinism*. Grand Rapids: Eerdmans, 1961.

_____. *The Practice of Godliness*. Grand Rapids: Eerdmans, 1945.

_____. *Pro Rege, of Het Koningschap van Christus*. 3 vols. Kampen: J. H. Kok, 1911–1912.

_____. *Souvereiniteit in Eigen Kring*. Amsterdam: J. H. Kruyt, 1880.

_____. *To Be Near unto God*. Grand Rapids: Eerdmans, 1924.

_____. *The Work of the Holy Spirit*. New York: Funk & Wagnalls, 1900.

3. 1890–1915

Berkhof, Louis. *The Church and Social Problems*. Grand Rapids: Eerdmans-Sevensma, 1913.

Gaffin, Richard B., Jr., ed. *Redemptive History and Biblical Interpretation: The Shorter Writings of Geerhardus Vos*. Philipsburg, NJ: Presbyterian and Reformed, 1980.

Hulst, Lammert J., and Hemkes, Gerrit K. *Oud- en Nieuw-Calvinisme: Tweeledige inlichting voor ons Hollandische Volk. . . .* Grand Rapids: Eerdmans-Sevensma, 1913.

Kuiper, Barend Klaas. *Ons Opmaken en Bouwen*. Grand Rapids: Eerdmans-Sevensma, 1918.

_____. *The Proposed Calvinistic College at Grand Rapids*. Grand Rapids: Sevensma, 1903.

Semi-Centennial Committee of the Christian Reformed Church. *Gedenkboek van het Vijftigjarig Jubileum der Christelijke Gereformeerde Kerk: A. D. 1857–1907*. Grand Rapids: Hulst-Sevensma, 1907.

Steffens, Nicholas M. "Calvinism and the Theological Crisis." *Presbyterian and Reformed Review* 12 (April 1901): 211–25.

Ten Hoor, Foppe M. Series on Americanization. *Gereformeerde Amerikaan* 2 (May-August 1898) and 13 (January-March, May, September 1909).

_____. Series Contra Supralapsarian/Neo-Calvinism. *Gereformeerde Amerikaan* 9 (May-September 1905) and 20 (February, May, July, September, October 1916).

_____. "De Moderne Positieve Theologie." *Gereformeerde Amerikaan* 12/13 (October 1908-January 1909).

_____. On Mysticism. *Gereformeerde Amerikaan* 1 (March-August 1897).

Van Lonkhuyzen, John. *Billy Sunday: Een Beeld uit het Tegenwoordige Amerikaansche Godsdienstige Leven*. Grand Rapids: Eerdmans-Sevensma, 1916.

4. 1915–1930

Berkhof, Louis. *De Drie Punten in Alle Deelen Gereformeerd*. Grand Rapids: Eerdmans, 1925.

_____. *Premillennialisme: Zijn Schriftuurlijke Basis en Enkele van zijn Practische Gevolgtrekkingen*. Grand Rapids: Eerdmans-Sevensma, 1918.

Berkhof, Louis et al. *Waar Het in de Zaak Janssen Om Gaat*. n.p., 1922.

Bultema, Harry. *Maranatha! Eene Studie over de Onvervulde Profetie*. Grand Rapids: Eerdmans-Sevensma, 1917.

Christian Reformed Church. *Reports and Decisions in the Case of Dr. R. Janssen*. Synod of Orange City, 1922.

De Jong, Ymen P. *Daden des Heeren: Drie Leerredenen Gehouden in verband met den Wereld Oorlog 1914–1919*. Grand Rapids: n.p., 1919.

_____. *De Komende Christus: Eene Studie ter Weerlegging van de Grondstellingen van het Pre-Millennialisme*. Grand Rapids: Van Noord, 1920.

Dosker, Henry E. *The Dutch Anabaptists*. Philadelphia: Judson, 1921.

Hoeksema, Gertrude. *Therefore Have I Spoken: A Biography of Herman Hoeksema*. Grand Rapids: Reformed Free Publishing Association, 1969.

Hoeksema, Herman. *The Protestant Reformed Churches in America: Their Origin, Early History, and Doctrine*. Grand Rapids: First Protestant Reformed Church, 1936.

_____. *Van Zonde en Genade*. Kalamazoo, MI: n.p. 1923.

Hoeksema, Herman, and Danhof, Henry. *Niet Doopersch Maar Gereformeerd*. n.p., 1922.

Hospers, Gerrit H. *The Reformed Principle of Authority*. Grand Rapids: Eerdmans, 1924.

Janssen, Ralph. *De Crisis in de Christelijke Gereformeerde Kerk in Amerika: Een Strijdschrift*. Grand Rapids: n.p., 1922.

_____. *De Synodale Conclusies*. Grand Rapids: n.p., 1923.

Kuiper, Barend K. *De Vier Paarden uit Openbaring.* Grand Rapids: Eerdmans-Sevensma, 1918.

Kuiper, Herman. *Calvin on Common Grace.* Goes: Oosterbaan & Le Cointre, 1928.

Kuiper, Rienck B. *"Not of the World": Discourses on the Christian's Relation to the World.* Grand Rapids: Eerdmans, 1929.

_____. *While the Bridegroom Tarries: Ten After-the-War Sermons on the Signs of the Times.* Grand Rapids: Van Noord, 1919.

Ten Hoor, Foppe M. et al. *Nadere Toelichting omtrent de Zaak Janssen.* Holland, MI: Holland Printing, 1920.

Van Baalen, Jan Karel. *De Loochening der Gemeene Gratie: Gereformeerd of Doopersch?* Grand Rapids: Eerdmans-Sevensma, 1922.

_____. *Nieuwigheid en Dwaling: De Loochening der Gemeene Gratie Nogmaals Gewogen en te Licht Bevonden.* Grand Rapids: Eerdmans-Sevensma, 1923.

Van Eyck, William O. *Landmarks of the Reformed Fathers: Or, What Van Raalte's People Really Believed.* Grand Rapids: Reformed Press, 1922.

Vos, Geerhardus. *The Self-Disclosure of Jesus.* New York: Doran, 1926.

5. 1930–1950

Beets, Henry. *The Man of Sorrows: A Series of Lenten Sermons.* Grand Rapids: Eerdmans, 1935.

Berkhof, Louis. *Aspects of Liberalism.* Grand Rapids: Eerdmans, 1951.

_____. *The Kingdom of God: The Development of the Idea of the Kingdom, Especially Since the Eighteenth Century.* Grand Rapids: Eerdmans, 1951.

_____. *Manual of Reformed Doctrine.* Grand Rapids: Eerdmans, 1933.

_____. *Reformed Dogmatics.* 3 vols. Grand Rapids: Eerdmans, 1932.

_____. *Riches of Divine Grace: Ten Expository Sermons.* Grand Rapids: Eerdmans, 1948.

_____. *Vicarious Atonement Through Christ.* Grand Rapids: Eerdmans, 1936.

Blekkink, Evert J. *The Fatherhood of God.* Grand Rapids: Eerdmans, 1942.

Blocker, Simon. *When Christ Takes Over.* Grand Rapids: Eerdmans, 1945.

Bouma, Clarence. "Calvinism in American Theology Today." *Journal of Religion* 27 (1947): 34–45.

_____. "Christianity's Finality and New Testament Teaching." *Princeton Theological Review* 26 (1928): 337-58.

_____. "War, Peace, and the Christian." *Calvin Forum* 1 (1935): 99–102.

DeBoer, Cecil. *The If's and Ought's of Ethics: A Preface to Moral Philosophy.* Grand Rapids: Eerdmans, 1936.

DeJong, Peter Y. *The Covenant Idea in New England Theology, 1620–1847.* Grand Rapids: Eerdmans, 1945.

DeVries, John. *Beyond the Atom: An Appraisal of Our Christian Faith in This Age of Atomic Science.* Grand Rapids: Eerdmans, 1948.

Hendriksen, William. *The Covenant of Grace.* Grand Rapids: Eerdmans, 1932.

_____. *More Than Conquerors: An Interpretation of the Book of Revelation*. Grand Rapids: Baker, 1940.

Kromminga, Dietrich H. *The Millennium in the Church: Studies in the History of Christian Chiliasm*. Grand Rapids: Eerdmans, 1945.

Kruithof, Bastian. *The Christ of the Cosmic Road: The Significance of the Incarnation*. Grand Rapids: Eerdmans, 1937.

_____. *The High Points of Calvinism*. Grand Rapids: Baker, 1949.

Kuizenga, John E. *Relevancy of the Pivot Points of the Reformed Faith*. Grand Rapids: Society for Reformed Publications, 1951.

Meeter, H. Henry. *Calvinism: An Interpretation of Its Basic Ideas*. Grand Rapids: Zondervan, 1939.

Pieters, Albertus. *The Facts and Mysteries of the Christian Faith*. Grand Rapids: Eerdmans, 1926.

_____. *Studies in the Revelation of St. John*. Grand Rapids: Eerdmans, 1954.

Tanis, Edward J. *Calvinism and Social Problems*. Grand Rapids: Zondervan, 1936.

Van Baalen, Jan Karel. *The Heritage of the Fathers*. Grand Rapids: Eerdmans, 1948.

Vos, Geerhardus. *Biblical Theology*. Grand Rapids: Eerdmans, 1948.

_____. *The Pauline Eschatology*. Princeton: Princeton University Press, 1930.

Wyngaarden, Martin J. *The Future of the Kingdom in Prophecy and Fulfillment: A Study of the Scope of "Spiritualization" in Scripture*. Grand Rapids: Zondervan, 1934.

6. 1950–1965

Boer, Harry R. *Pentecost and Missions*. Grand Rapids: Eerdmans, 1961.

Bruggink, Donald, ed. *Guilt, Grace, and Gratitude: A Commentary on the Heidelberg Catechism*. New York: Half Moon, 1963.

Buis, Harry. *The Doctrine of Eternal Punishment*. Philadelphia: Presbyterian and Reformed, 1957.

Daane, James. *A Theology of Grace*. Grand Rapids: Eerdmans, 1954.

_____. *The Freedom of God: A Study of Election and Pulpit*. Grand Rapids: Eerdmans, 1973.

De Boer, Cecil. *Responsible Protestantism*. Grand Rapids: Eerdmans, 1957.

DeJong, Alexander C. *The Well-Meant Gospel Offer: The Views of K. Schilder and H. Hoeksema*. Franeker: Wever, 1954.

DeJong, Peter Y. *The Church's Witness to the World*. Grand Rapids: Baker, 1960.

Dekker, Harold. "On the Doctrine of Limited Atonement." *Reformed Journal* 12–14 (December 1962–March 1963; January–March, May, September 1964).

DeKoster, Lester. *All Ye That Labor: An Essay on Christianity, Communism, and the Problem of Evil*. Grand Rapids: Eerdmans, 1956.

Girod, Gordon. *The Deeper Faith*. Grand Rapids: Reformed Publications, 1958.

Hageman, Howard. *Pulpit and Table: Some Chapters in the History of Worship in the Reformed Churches*. Richmond: John Knox, 1962.

Klooster, Fred. *The Significance of Barth's Theology: An Appraisal*. Grand Rapids: Baker, 1961.

Kuiper, Rienck Bouke. *God-Centered Evangelism*. Grand Rapids: Baker, 1961.

_____. *For Whom Did Christ Die?* Grand Rapids: Eerdmans, 1959.

_____. *To Be or Not to Be Reformed: Whither the Christian Reformed Church?* Grand Rapids: Zondervan, 1959.

Masselink, William. *General Revelation and Common Grace*. Grand Rapids: Eerdmans, 1953.

Stob, Henry. *The Christian Conception of Freedom*. Grand Rapids: Grand Rapids International Publications, 1957.

Van Til, Cornelius. *Common Grace*. Philadelphia: Presbyterian and Reformed, 1947.

Van Til, Henry R. *The Calvinistic Concept of Culture*. Grand Rapids: Baker, 1959.

Verduin, Leonard. *The Reformers and Their Stepchildren*. Grand Rapids: Eerdmans, 1964.

Zylstra, Henry. *Testament of Vision*. Grand Rapids: Eerdmans, 1958.

7. Since 1965

Bril, K. A., Hart, Hendrik, and Klapwijk, Jacob, eds. *The Idea of a Christian Philosophy: Essays in Honor of H. Th. Vollenhoven*. Toronto: Wedge, 1973.

Boer, Harry R. *Above the Battle? The Bible and Its Critics*. Grand Rapids: Eerdmans, 1977.

_____. *The Doctrine of Reprobation in the Christian Reformed Church*. Grand Rapids: Eerdmans, 1983.

Bruggink, Donald. *When Faith Takes Form*. Grand Rapids: Eerdmans, 1971.

Christian Reformed Church. *The Nature and Extent of Biblical Authority*. Grand Rapids: Board of Publications of the CRC, 1972.

De Jong, Peter Y., ed. *Crisis in the Reformed Churches: Essays in Commemoration of the Great Synod of Dort, 1618-1619*. Grand Rapids: Reformed Fellowship, 1968.

Hart, Hendrik. *The Challenge of Our Age*. Toronto: Wedge, 1974.

_____. *Understanding Our World: An Integrated Ontology*. Lanham, MD: University Press of America, 1984.

Hart, Hendrik, van der Hoeven, Johan, and Wolterstorff, Nicholas, eds. *Rationality in the Calvinian Tradition*. Lanham, MD: University Press of America, 1983.

Heideman, Eugene P. *Our Song of Hope: A Provisional Confession of Faith of the Reformed Churches in America*. Grand Rapids: Eerdmans, 1975.

Hoekema, Anthony. *The Christian Looks at Himself*. Grand Rapids: Eerdmans, 1975.

_____. *Holy Spirit Baptism*. Grand Rapids: Eerdmans, 1972.

Kalsbeek, L. *Contours of a Christian Philosophy*. Toronto: Wedge, 1975.

Kistemaker, Simon. *Interpreting God's Word Today*. Grand Rapids: Baker, 1970.

Kraay, John, and Tol, Anthony, eds. *Hearing and Doing: Philosophical Essays Dedicated to H. Evan Runner*. Toronto: Wedge, 1979.

Kuyper, Lester. *The Scripture Unbroken*. Grand Rapids: Eerdmans, 1978.

McIntire, C. Thomas, ed. *The Legacy of Herman Dooyeweerd*. Lanham, MD: University Press of America, 1985.

Mouw, Richard J. *Called to Holy Worldliness*. Philadelphia: Fortress, 1980.

_____. *Political Evangelism*. Grand Rapids: Eerdmans, 1974.

_____. *Politics and the Biblical Drama*. Grand Rapids: Eerdmans, 1976.

Olthuis, John A. et al. *Out of Concern for the Church*. Toronto: Wedge, 1970.

Osterhaven, M. Eugene. *The Faith of the Church*. Grand Rapids: Eerdmans, 1971.

_____. *The Spirit of the Reformed Tradition*. Grand Rapids: Eerdmans, 1982.

Plantinga, Alvin. *God and Other Minds: A Study of the Rational Justification of Belief in God*. Ithaca: Cornell University Press, 1967.

_____. *God, Freedom, and Evil*. New York: Harper & Row, 1974.

_____, ed. *Faith and Philosophy*. Grand Rapids: Eerdmans, 1964.

Plantinga, Alvin, and Wolterstorff, Nicholas, eds. *Faith and Rationality: Reason and Belief in God*. Notre Dame: University of Notre Dame Press, 1983.

Plantinga, Cornelius. *A Place to Stand: A Reformed Study of Creeds and Confessions*. Grand Rapids: Board of Publications of the CRC, 1979.

Runner, H. Evan. *The Relation of the Bible to Learning*. 3d ed. Toronto: Wedge, 1970.

_____. *Scriptural Religion and the Political Task*. 3d ed. Toronto: Wedge, 1974.

Smedes, Lewis B. *All Things Made New: A Theology of Man's Union with Christ*. Grand Rapids: Eerdmans, 1970.

_____. *Love Within Limits: A Realist's View of 1 Corinthians 13*. Grand Rapids: Eerdmans, 1978.

_____. *Mere Morality: What God Expects from Ordinary People*. Grand Rapids: Eerdmans, 1983.

Stob, Henry. *Ethical Reflections*. Grand Rapids: Eerdmans, 1978.

Vander Goot, Henry, ed. *Life Is Religion: Essays in Honor of H. Evan Runner*. St. Catharines, Ontario: Paideia, 1981.

Vander Stelt, John. *Philosophy and Scripture: A Study in Old Princeton and Westminster Theology*. Marlton, NJ: Mack, 1978.

Van Til, Howard J. *The Fourth Day: What the Bible and the Heavens Are Telling Us about the Creation*. Grand Rapids: Eerdmans, 1986.

Wolterstorff, Nicholas. *Art in Action*. Grand Rapids: Eerdmans, 1980.

_____. *Reason Within the Bounds of Religion*. Grand Rapids: Eerdmans, 1976.

_____. *Until Justice and Peace Embrace*. Grand Rapids: Eerdmans, 1983.

INDEX